Brian Powley

Scotland .

May 1968 .

New Directions in Theology Today

VOLUME II

History and Hermeneutics

New Directions in Theology Today
WILLIAM HORDERN, GENERAL EDITOR

VOL. I INTRODUCTION
BY WILLIAM HORDERN

VOL. II HISTORY AND HERMENEUTICS
BY CARL E. BRAATEN

VOL. III GOD
BY JOHN MACQUARRIE

VOL. IV THE CHURCH
BY COLIN WILLIAMS

VOL. V CHRISTIAN LIFE
BY PAUL HESSERT

VOL. VI MAN
BY ROGER L. SHINN

VOL. VII CHRIST
BY ROBERT CLYDE JOHNSON

NEW DIRECTIONS IN THEOLOGY TODAY

Volume II
History
and
Hermeneutics

BY
CARL E. BRAATEN

London
Lutterworth Press

IN MEMORY OF MY TEACHER

PAUL J. TILLICH

Editor's Foreword

Theology always has existed in some tension with the church. But there is considerable evidence that today the gulf is wider than ever before. To both pastors and laymen it often seems that contemporary theology is working in opposition to the concerns of the parish. They are disturbed to read in newspapers and popular journals about theologians who seem to have lightly cast aside the cornerstones of the faith and who argue that the parish is doomed. To the theologian the parish often appears to be a respectable club dedicated to erecting buildings, raising budgets, and avoiding controversial issues.

There is little active dialogue between the theologian and the church today. The fault for this lies with both parties, but the situation is becoming increasingly serious as the church moves into a new age. This series is dedicated to the task of bridging the present gulf.

One of the reasons for the gulf between theology and the church is that neither the busy pastor nor the concerned layman can keep up to date with an ever-expanding theological literature. Thus, the purpose of New Directions in Theology Today is to present concise summaries of the present scene in theology. The series is not for the lazy pastor, nor for the layman who is beginning his theological education. Rather, these volumes are especially prepared for the busy pastor who is concerned with keeping abreast of modern theology and for the layman who, having been initiated into theology, is reading for further study, particularly to find out what contemporary Christian thinkers are saying.

The series is not written with the assumption that only professional theologians have something to say, but is offered in the hope that it will stimulate pastors and laymen to enter into the theological dialogue, and with the conviction that a vital theology for our time must be the work of the church as a whole.

WILLIAM HORDERN

Contents

CHAPTER I

The Idea of Revelation Through History

THE INFLATION OF REVELATION

Roman Catholic theology today is catching up with Protestant theology; it is no longer sure of what it means by revelation. Ever since the decline of Protestant orthodoxy, theology has been in search of a category by which to define revelation. The search continues today. At no point do the antitheses in theology become more clearly displayed than in the doctrine of revelation. At Vatican Council II, the Roman bishops and their theologians debated the question of the *sources* of revelation. Is God's revelation contained *partly* in Scripture and *partly* in tradition, or can all of it be found in Scripture? Protestant theology, however, has put the question about revelation in a much more radical way. Where can revelation be found at all, now that the traditional equation of Scripture with revelation can no longer stand unchallenged in the face of the historical criticism of the Bible? What category of experience leads us to the root of revelation underlying the layers of tradition documented in the Scripture itself?

The intense search for a category that locates revelation is impelled by the widespread assumption in Protestant theology that the idea of revelation itself most comprehensively and profoundly expresses the uniqueness of the Christian faith. Every modern Protestant theology, regardless of which category shapes its thinking, has felt obliged to establish itself as a theology of revelation, as if thereby it has achieved all that matters or what matters most. There is no doubt that any theology which deserves to be called Christian will include the notion that man's knowledge of God presupposes God's revelation of himself. We can know God only when, where, and how he reveals himself. But it does not follow from this that the idea of revelation expresses either the depths or the totality of the uniquely Christian message. Paul Althaus, emeritus professor of systematic theology at Erlangen University, long ago called attention to the inflation of the concept of revelation in contemporary theology.[1] This inflation can best be explained by the heightened epistemological consciousness that was introduced into theology by Immanuel Kant's critiques of reason. Modern man—whoever he is—seems less concerned with *what* the theologian has to say than whether he can say *anything* at all. The question "How do you know?" is always the first question the theologian is asked. Thus, when the problem of religious knowledge becomes central in theology, the idea of revelation, as the answer to this question, becomes correspondingly dominant.

The dominance of the idea of revelation in modern theology is clearly exhibited by the *Church Dogmatics* of Karl Barth. Popular opinion has it that Karl Barth, unlike Paul Tillich, does not start his theology with the question of modern man, but goes back to the Bible by way of the Reformation. Nothing could be more misleading. When Paul Tillich begins his *Systematic Theology* with the epistemological part, "Reason and Revelation," he grants that this is a concession to the modern question, "On what do you base your assertions; what criteria, what verification do you have?"[2] Not so with Karl Barth! He claims that the order of questions which dogmatics treats must be determined by the framework given by the divine revelation itself. God's questions, not man's, must predominate. Modern man with his questions must not be allowed to fix the framework and write the agenda for theology.

Gustaf Wingren, successor of Anders Nygren at Lund, Sweden, has called this Barthian claim to theocentricity into question in his polemical writing *Theology in Conflict*.[3] The inflationary development of the concept of revelation in Barth's theology has as its unavowed presupposition the portrait of the modern agnostic with his lack of the knowledge of God. While Barth wants to make God the center of his theology, he has really made man the center. The entire activity of the triune God is subsumed under the rubric of revelation, thereby implicitly setting theology into the epistemological straitjacket of the modern man who, with a nod from Karl Barth, thinks he knows nothing about God. The Godless man, the theological ignoramus, the fool of Ps. 53, is in a predicament; he knows nothing of God. He does not even know that God exists. His lack of knowledge governs the response of theology. Theology accepts the word of the atheist at face value, and reestablishes the knowledge of God solely on a special revelation, privy to members of an esoteric society with their own in-group symbols of language. If this is the best that theology can do today, it ought at least to be acknowledged as a new, and rather desperate, apologetic maneuver of church theology in the face of an embarrassment.

There are, moreover, serious reservations that must be voiced against the dominant position of the idea of revelation in theology, with its corollary that man's essential predicament is his lack of knowledge. There is, first, the fact that neither the Bible, nor the Reformation, nor the broad stream of catholic tradition, has ever so conceived of the God-man relationship. It is definitely a twentieth-century phenomenon, with nineteenth-century roots in the Kant-Ritschl line of thought. And the theology of Karl Barth can be seen as the *ne plus ultra* of this type of thinking. If the ignorance of man stands in the center, then the fact of revelation relieves that plight; but if man's *guilt* is the problem, then not revelation but *reconciliation* must become the theological centrum. Secondly, when the idea of revelation is the controlling perspective, Jesus Christ is identified as the self-revelation of God, and in Barth's theology, as the sole revelation of God. Jesus Christ functions primarily as a bridge, the only bridge, between God's revelation and man's ignorance.

We have several serious reservations about this christo-monistic idea of revelation. A fair attention to the Biblical evidence will show, in the first place, that Jesus Christ is not the sole medium of revelation and, in the second place, that much more than revelation was accomplished by him. To be sure, God revealed himself in Jesus of Nazareth, but not first and only in him. No adequate account of the Old Testament is possible as long as Christology holds a monopoly on revelation; and, likewise, no adequate grasp of the significance of Jesus Christ is possible as long as revelation is the leading explanatory concept. If the special status of Jesus Christ must be explicated by the term "revelation," then we are driven either to deny that God reveals himself elsewhere, as Barth has done to uphold the uniqueness of Christ, or to reduce Jesus Christ to the level of other revelations, as liberal theology has done with its "low" Christology. There is a way out of this dilemma. It lies in the proper distinction between revelation and salvation.

There is a twofold revelation of God: through the law of creation and through the gospel of Christ. There is the revelation not only of God's love but also of his justice (and wrath). The direct, unique, and unsurpassable revelation of God's love in Christ is preceded by the indirect revelation of God's will in the political and existential spheres of life. Our purpose here is not to defend or develop this view of the dual character of divine revelation. Emil Brunner fought this battle against Karl Barth in the thirties, and despite Barth's greater dialectical dexterity, later theology has on the whole vindicated Brunner's position which asserts a double revelation against the mono-Christological view of Barthianism.

Given the dual character of revelation, it is impossible for the category of revelation to bring out more than a difference in degree between Christ and others. And since this reduction of Christ to the level of others violates the integrity of Christian faith, Barth was forced to reject every other revelation. Then Christ stands unique—alone! Accepting the same options for ourselves, we would have to judge him in the right. By distinguishing revelation and reconciliation, however, it is possible to maintain both the duality of revelation and the uniqueness of Christ. Jesus Christ is the sole Savior, not the sole revealer. The idea of revelation suggests that something is disclosed that was previously hidden. The Christ event is not a disclosure of something that has always been but that has hitherto remained hidden and shrouded in mystery. That is a completely Platonic view of revelation. Rather, something new *happens* in Christ, the act of reconciliation. Reconciliation is not merely revealed, as if it were there but only hidden;

it is acted out in history, a unique event, something absolutely new under the sun. Revelation goes primarily to the consciousness and makes the faith a rather cerebral affair; the act of reconciliation brings about an objectively new situation, not just for the believer but for the cosmos. The *world* was reconciled to God in Christ. The dramatic, historical character of the Christ event tends to be diminished by the inflation of revelation as an answer to the hypersensitive epistemological consciousness of modern theology. And it is thereby assumed that the questions of reconciliation and forgiveness for guilt and sin are no longer the central human questions; they have been removed to make room for the single, all-consuming interest in the question of knowledge. No doubt theology will have to take seriously the modern question of religious *knowledge,* but it should not assume that because this is *the* twentieth-century question, it is necessarily the profoundest one, nor the one that correlates best with the heart of the Biblical message.

THE ASCENDANCY OF HISTORY

What we have said about revelation in the interests of a critical theological self-consciousness must also be said in the face of the ascendancy of the category of history in current thinking. The coupling of revelation with history is an omnipresent feature of modern theology. It is almost unthinkable that revelation could be mediated except through something called historical events or historical existence.

The category of history is undoubtedly indispensable for a theology based on God's reconciling activity in Christ. The act of reconciliation is a climactic historical event, with definite historical presuppositions in Yahweh's covenant with Israel and equally definite historical results in the election of the church. To the extent that the redemption through Christ is taken seriously, history must be given its due. There is an irreducible kernel of truth in the refrain that Christianity is a historical religion. But what justification is there for reducing all the media of revelation to history? Why must all talk about revelation answer to the requirements of history? Is the idea of history really capable of exhausting what the Scriptures mean by revelation?

Already, one theologian has issued a caveat against the belief that history is the only channel of divine revelation. James Barr, in his inaugural address at Princeton Theological Seminary,[4] expressed the conviction, which he admitted would sound like the archheresy for modern theology, that the formula "revelation through history" cannot be our only hermeneutical guideline without doing violence to the Biblical texts. It is impossible to subsume all the Biblical evidence under "revelation through history." To support this assertion, Barr offers two quite irrefutable facts. The first is that in the whole Wisdom Literature, God is not seen as communicating with men through special historical events. The examples he cites are Proverbs, Ecclesiastes, and Psalms. "There are substantial areas of the Old Testament which do not support and do not fit in with the idea that revelation through history is the fundamental motif of Old Testament thought."[5] Secondly, according to the self-understanding of the Biblical narrators of the exodus event, God revealed his will to his people not only through the event itself but before, during, and after this event, he entered into a direct verbal conversation with his prophet Moses. It would appear then that God's way of declaring himself is much too complex to allow its reduction to a single, simple formula.

These reservations about the formula "revelation

through history" do not invalidate the concept. While James Barr is right in pointing out that history is not a Biblical category, the matter itself is present in the Bible. But more important than the use of the category is the sense in which it is being used. Every theologian will tie revelation to history in some way, but behind an apparent consensus lurks a wide divergency of meaning. The tensions that exist today between the *Heilsgeschichte* and existentialist theologians arise from their totally different views of history. These tensions will be pointed up in every chapter of this book. The fact, however, that both sides clutch this term as the be-all and end-all of Christian theology, while meaning vastly different things by it, must be a sign of something. Barr detects here a response to an apologetic need to demonstrate that, in an age of historical consciousness, the Christian faith takes history in utter seriousness, and is quite able to meet the challenge of historical relativism and apply the critical methods of historical science without committing suicide.

This apologetic need to square the essentials of faith with the perspectives of history was first powerfully felt in the nineteenth century. Therefore, to understand better the present throes of theology as it teeters between existentialist and *Heilsgeschichte* interpretations of revelation and history, we will present a rapid sketch of earlier oscillations in nineteenth-century thought.

Nineteenth-Century Ideas of Revelation

When Immanuel Kant placed revelation within the limits of reason alone, he was acting as a true spokesman of the Enlightenment. In his book *Religion Within the Limits of Reason Alone,* Kant offers only three options on the question of revelation: naturalism, which denies every supernatural revelation of God; rationalism, which accepts historical revelation, but only as a provisional stage on the way to a religion of reason; and supernaturalism, which holds to the necessity of a religion revealed in a super-natural way and its superiority over every natural religion.[6] Nineteenth-century theology can be seen as a struggle to liberate religion from its bondage to any of these options. Orthodox supernaturalism had become as rationalistic as its Enlightenment critics, with its view of Biblical revela-tion as a sum of true doctrinal propositions. Dogmatic theology had only to bring order out of the chaotic form in which the Holy Spirit had placed these propositions in the Bible.

Liberation from the hegemony of eighteenth-century rationalism came in two different forms: Johann Gottfried Herder's (1744–1803) theology of history and Friedrich Schleiermacher's (1768–1834) theology of experience.

In Herder's thought, we can trace the beginnings of German historicism which undergo a series of modifica-tions through classical German idealism (Hegel and Schel-ling), the *Heilsgeschichte* theology of the Erlangen School (J. C. K. von Hofmann), Wilhelm Dilthey's philosophy of historical relativism, and the history of religions school most eminently represented by Ernst Troeltsch. Today it is being revived in a highly modified way in the new theological school associated with the name of Wolfhart Pannenberg. This school attempts to free the category of history from the naturalistic, positivistic determinants from which it suffered in its late nineteenth-century applica-tions in Biblical research.

Not all scholars mean the same thing by "historicism." In modern theology, however, it has generally become a bad word because we have happened to know it chiefly in its positivistic form. It was against positivistic historicism that the dialectical theologians in the early twenties issued their protests. At that time the historical interpretation of the Biblical revelation was controlled by an immanentalist, evolutionary world view, by the liberal idea of progress, and by historical methods modeled after the empirical methodology of the natural sciences. But in its classical prepositivistic form, historicism contained elements in its vision which have become the common property of every theological school today.

We are all indebted to the historical way of thinking. In fact, modern theology began with the entrance of historical concerns in theology, and the exit of a dogmatic way of thinking riveted to the unhistorical ontology of Aristotelian scholasticism that ran through all theology from the thirteenth through the seventeenth century. History has become our fate, and, like it or not, theology will persist in correlating history with revelation in one way or another. Traditionally, theology has known a variety of media of revelation.[7] Modern theology, however, seems fated to make its case for revelation at the bar of history. In another period some other category may become the point at which battle lines are drawn.

If the genius of historicism was its view of a dynamic, progressive revelation working its way through the particulars of history and coming to expression in ever-changing forms of thought, its crucial liability was its tendency to make revelation a predicate of a universal historical process. The result was that the radical creatureliness of history became absorbed in a historical pantheism, the uniqueness of the Biblical revelation became relativized, and the once-for-all character of the eschatological event in Christ was juggled away. If the historical approach must lead to such consequences, Christian theologians might be willing to bypass history altogether, or at least push it into a corner where it can do no harm—precisely what happened in the dialectical theology. The present disenchantment with the theologies of Barth and Bultmann has arisen in the name of "taking history seriously." They are being accused of rescuing revelation by removing it from the sphere that ordinary men call history. That this disenchantment takes on different aspects, whether oriented to Barth or Bultmann, does not gainsay the charge that they abandoned history to the historians and made room for a theology of revelation at the frayed edges of history.

In the case of the early Barth, revelation was posited in a sphere that he called *Urgeschichte* (prehistory), whereas Bultmann retreated with his revelation into the area of existential meaning in the historicity (*Geschichtlichkeit*) of the individual. In fairness to Barth, it must be acknowledged that as the writing of the *Church Dogmatics* progressed, he not only abandoned his earlier idea of *Urgeschichte* but more and more resumed friendly relations with traditional *Heilsgeschichte* theology. The language of history plays an increasingly preponderant role in his thinking.

If Barth has veered more toward a historical view of revelation, Bultmann has remained faithful to an existentialist theology to which he committed himself early in his development. Contrary to the opinion of many Bultmann scholars, contemporary existentialist theology is not a twentieth-century novelty. Its roots can be traced back to the second major alternative to orthodox and Enlightenment rationalism, namely, Schleiermacher's mystical theology of religious experience. Existentialism is the present-day edition of mysticism. Both are guilty of a massive interiorization of the Biblical historical drama of salvation. That is a thesis which is by no means self-evident. The symptoms of their continuity become most apparent in Christology, which is constructed, not forward from the Old Testament anticipations of historical fulfillment, but backward from the existential realization of salvation in the individual believer. Christology becomes the reflexive action of a pious self-consciousness (Schleiermacher) or an existential self-understanding (Bultmann) accounting for the peculiar qualities of its own sense of beatitude (grace), with recourse to the New Testament as a document in which this understanding first and most purely came to expression. The *now* of salvation in the immediacy of experience is, at any rate, accentuated at the expense of the past and future historical referents in the drama of salvation.

Schleiermacher's definition of revelation as an original impression made by a person "upon the self-consciousness of those into whose circle he enters"[3] was the basis of his theology of experience. Theology is a description of the states of self-awareness. This starting point of theology suffered a fate similar to Herder's theology of history. As the latter evolved into an "ism" (historicism), Schleiermacher's theology of pious self-awareness quickly degenerated into a psychologism, with most telling effects upon the Life of Jesus movement. And another result of this psychologism was the suspension of the category of faith in a state of fine diffusion in religious experiences. The Barthian revolution in theology was thus equally as concerned to rescue faith from the psychology of religion as to redeem revelation from bondage to a philosophy of history.

Presented with two live options in overcoming dogmatic and moralistic types of rationalism, nineteenth-century theologians oscillated between the historical and psychological poles of religious knowledge. Numerous attempts were made to mediate between them. Revelation could be seen as an ellipse with two foci, the objective manifestation in history in union with the inspired interpretation of religious experience. The Erlangen School offered a brilliant synthesis of the historical and psychological modes of approach to revelation. J. C. K. von Hofmann represented more the historical motif and F. H. R. von Frank more the experiential motif. Somewhat later, Hermann Cremer, Martin Kähler, and Adolph Schlatter tried to merge the horizons of Biblical *Heilsgeschichte* with the experience of justifying faith. In their definition of revelation they kept real historical facts indissolubly together with the accompanying word of interpretation. Facts without words are blind; and words without facts are empty, to paraphrase one of Kant's famous utterances. God reveals himself in history in such a way that both the facts and the words are seen as his acts. Against historicism they stressed the suprahistorical character of revelation, and against psychologism (or subjectivism) they reasserted the Reformation faith that the words of man can become the Word of God through the agency of the Holy Spirit, and therefore something more than mere utterances of religious feelings.

The theology of revelation of the Biblical systematicians like Kähler and Schlatter—often called "Biblicists" by their opponents—was inundated by the flood tides of historicism and subjectivism at the turn of the century. The idea of revelation as the mighty acts of God in history, transmitted through a uniquely inspired medium of interpretation by prophets and apostles, was radically swept aside by leading historical critics. The initiative had shifted to the fields of church history and the history of religions. Adolf von Harnack and Ernst Troeltsch were the magnates of university theology; the comparative study of religions was the queen of the sciences. Dogmatics was in bad shape. Troeltsch could say: "Dogmatics is a discipline which exists today only in the narrowest of theological circles, and even there it languishes."[9]

The historical studies did not lead to a renewed confidence in the reality and truth of the Christian revelation. The historical-critical method fossilized the Biblical message. History was proving to be a very questionable handle by which to lay hold of revelation. So the stage was set for the sudden appearance of dialectical theology. Many factors contributed to its meteoric success. Not least among them was a profound ennui among theological students in the face of the purely historical mode of thought and its prevailing relativizing effects. On January 1, 1916, in a letter to his friend Eduard Thurneysen, Karl Barth expressed the then emerging mood perfectly: "How frightfully indifferent I have become about the purely historical questions. Of course, that is nothing new for me. Already under the influence of Herrmann, I always thought of historical criticism as merely a means of attaining freedom in relation to the tradition, not, however, as a constituting factor in a new liberal tradition."[10]

Karl Barth's indifference to historical questions was consistent with his transcendental view of revelation and faith. The Calvinist Christological axiom, *finitum non capax infiniti* (the finite is not capable of the infinite), was expanded by Barth into a static dialectical principle opposing revelation to history. Revelation touches history as a tangent touches a circle. There is nothing in history on which faith could base itself, for faith is a vacuum filled not from history below, but from revelation above. Friedrich Gogarten, Emil Brunner, and Rudolf Bultmann joined Karl Barth in defining revelation and faith negatively in relation to history. Before them Martin Kähler had repudiated the idea that revelation could be historically verified, as supernaturalistic historicism (Ernst Hengstenberg) hoped, but he never intended to loosen the links between revelation and historical happenings as such. Now the dialectical team turned with vengeance upon history and began to talk so much about the "Word of God" (Barth) or the "kerygma" (Bultmann) or "personal encounter" (E. Brunner) or the "I-thou relationship" (Gogarten) that historical concerns were submerged beneath an avalanche of theological rhetoric.

The "theology of the Word" had its direct antecedent in Martin Kähler's stress on the kerygmatic intention of the Biblical texts. It was also nurtured by the Luther renaissance, and fortified by the form-critical study of the Gospels. Rudolf Bultmann's kerygma theology can be seen as the purest expression of a strictly consistent theology of the Word. It had some distinct advantages. The idea of the kerygma offered a new key to the interpretation of Scripture. Rationalism had looked for universal truths of reason; historicism searched for the factual links in an unbroken chain of cause and effect; and psychologism read the documents as samples of human religiosity. Bultmann's kerygma theology rested its case on the insight that the Scriptures are confessional documents; they witness to the saving act of God; they preach the gospel; they are written from faith unto faith. The idea of the kerygma prevented this theology from being classified and dismissed as just old-fashioned liberalism with a new jingo. But it was also a radical iconoclastic movement, tearing down the idols that nineteenth-century man had erected in the form of "isms" to encase the Word of God. Revelation was played off against reason, the kerygma against history, and faith against religion. Could Christian theology really tolerate for long this sort of radical bifurcation of reality? Doesn't radicalism thrive in a split world? In casting down the "isms," did not theology also throw away essential categories which the "isms" had distorted? Rational truths, historical facts, religious experiences—of what relevance could these be to theology? Theology has to do with the Word of God, with the kerygmatic Christ; so went the refrain!

REVELATION AS HISTORY

Modern theology is witnessing a revolt against an exclusive theology of the kerygma. Wolfhart Pannenberg, a youthful and prolific systematic theologian of the University of Mainz, together with a group of younger men teaching at other universities,[11] was the first to make an all-out assault on the positions of Barth and Bultmann. The battle cry is that the kerygma without history is a meaningless noise. The preaching of the "Word of God" is an empty assertion if it is severed from what really happened in history. Faith cannot live from a kerygma detached from its historical basis and content. For what is the kerygma but the declaration of what God has really done in the actual course of events out in the open where men and nations live and move?

Of course, the idea that the kerygma is linked to history has been for a long time a favorite theme of *Heilsgeschichte* theologians. Warnings against the loss of history have been repeatedly issued by theologians like Oscar

Cullmann[12] and Paul Althaus.[13] But these warnings have been mostly laughed off as not to be taken too seriously—like going at tigers with BB guns. While they affirmed a revelation *in* history, others thought it sounded like an arbitrary postulate of faith. Standard *Heilsgeschichte* theology, in the judgment of Pannenberg and his colleagues, failed to show how revelation and history are connected. It foundered on a dualism: revelation being assigned to the sphere of faith, and history to the methods of historical research. It never became clear how critical-historical research could serve the kerygma in transmitting, in a unified way, the revelatory and historical sides of the Biblical tradition. The epistemology of historical revelation, the issue we have broached here, has become the axial point in modern debate, and will claim our attention in the next chapter.

Wolfhart Pannenberg and his friends have published a symposium entitled *Revelation as History*.[14] The word "as" gives a clue to their ontology of historical revelation. What is the connection between revelation and history? Revelation comes not merely *in* or *through* history but *as* history. Revelation does not exist above history, entering it from the outside as a suprahistorical substance. Pannenberg agrees with Friedrich Gogarten and Rudolf Bultmann that the old ghost of supernaturalism hides behind the concept of the "suprahistorical."[15] But he goes farther and accuses them of substituting their own idea of the "eschatological" for the "suprahistorical" in an even more ruthless antithesis to historical reality.

Commentators on modern theology have habitually viewed the theologies of Barth and Bultmann as the two opposite ends of the theological spectrum. From the point of view of Pannenberg's interpretation of the problematic of historical revelation, both of them stand on the same side. Here is what he says: "Both theological positions, that of pure historicity and that of the supra-historical ground of faith, have a common extra-theological motive. Their common starting point is to be seen in the fact that critical-historical investigation as the scientific verification of events did not seem to leave any more room for redemptive events. Therefore the theology of redemptive history fled into a harbor supposedly safe from the critical-historical flood tide, the harbor of a supra-history—or with Barth, of prehistory. For the same reason the theology of existence withdrew from the meaningless and godless course of 'objective' history to the experience of the significance of history in the 'historicity' of the individual. The historical character of redemptive events must therefore be asserted today in discussion with the theology of existence, with the theology of redemptive history, and with the methodological principles of critical-historical investigation."[16] A telling confirmation of Pannenberg's discovery of a deep underlying kinship between Barth and Bultmann is the fact that their disciples have tended to bury their differences in the face of the threat posed by a new third force. Pannenberg's theology offers a real alternative to Barthianism or Bultmannianism, and to the various mediating options in between now being proposed by Gerhard Ebeling or Heinrich Ott.

In *Offenbarung als Geschichte,* Pannenberg summarizes his position in seven dogmatic theses on the doctrine of revelation. It is well to have them before us now as a basis for more detailed interpretation in pursuant chapters.

Thesis 1: According to the Biblical witnesses, the self-revelation of God has not occurred directly, after the fashion of a theophany, but indirectly through his historical acts.

Thesis 2: Revelation happens, not at the beginning, but at the end of history.

Thesis 3: Unlike special manifestations of God, historical revelation *is there* for anyone who has eyes to see. It is universal in character.

Thesis 4: The universal revelation of the Godhead of God was not yet realized in the history of Israel, but first in the destiny of Jesus of Nazareth insofar as the end of history occurs beforehand in him.

Thesis 5: The Christ event does not reveal the Godhead of the God of Israel as an isolated event, but only so far as it is part of God's history with Israel.

Thesis 6: The universality of the eschatological self-disclosure of God in the destiny of Jesus was expressed by using non-Jewish ideas of revelation in the instruction in Gentile Christian churches.

Thesis 7: The relation of the Word to revelation is in terms of prophecy, instruction, and report.[17]

The accent on the universal historical scope of revelation is a new departure in modern theology. It overcomes the cleavage between salvation history and world history that has been a common feature of both *Heilsgeschichte* and existentialist views of revelation. It undercuts the dualistic idea that an extraneous revelation touches upon our secular history at this point and that point or, as it were, flashes in upon an individual's existence as he stands upon a theologically neutral or irrelevant platform of history. The totality of reality as history is God's world which he creates and through which he reveals himself. The living God of the Bible is the Lord of the nations, not a local, tribal deity of Israel.

The motif of revelation as a universal historical process is reminiscent of Hegel's philosophy of history. Indeed, Pannenberg is being accused of a relapse into Hegelianism.[18] The connection between them is a real one, but not for that reason a discredit to either. And, in any case, Pannenberg's critical modifications of Hegel's system in the light of Biblical eschatology and Christology are not inconsiderable.

It often happens in the history of theology that a leap forward can be made only by taking a step backward. A step back to a unified theological understanding of reality as history may help to bridge a gap as wide as the history of modern theology is long. First there was G. E. Lessing with his "ugly ditch" between universal truths of reason and accidental truths of history; then came Johann Fichte's aphorism, "It is only the Metaphysical and on no account the Historical which makes blessed."[19] Later in the century neo-Kantianism drove a wedge between the noumenal and the phenomenal, between being and act, ontology and ethics, ontic judgments (*Seinsurteil*) and value judgments (*Werturteil*); theology had to decide which side of the world it wanted to hang on to. The trend continued, until Søren Kierkegaard's protest against Hegel in the name of the individual announced the subjectivity of truth, making faith a leap into the void—or one might even dare in fear and trembling to call it "God." The point is that the world was split; the church and its theology were quarantined in one corner, which has been getting smaller and smaller, until today the church is desperately struggling to regain contact with the world from which it has become alienated.

What will come of the attempt to put theology back on the rail by beginning again with Hegel's universal historical outlook remains to be seen. But, in a way, that is beside the point. What counts is whether theology has its eyes opened to a Biblical interpretation of history. Hegel, who tried to be true to the Biblical tradition, might be a help in that regard. Admittedly, that sounds strange to a generation suckled on Kierkegaard's anti-Hegelian pathos. But Kierkegaard can be seen as a corrective of Hegelian *hybris,* not necessarily a systemic substitute. Pannenberg too puts great store by Kierkegaard's corrections of Hegel, such as taking seriously the finitude of human existence, its limitations of knowledge, openness to a still unfinished and unpredictable future, and the irreplaceable uniqueness of the individual. The most serious failure of Hegel, and the one from which others derived, was to identify the end of history with his own system of philosophy. This was not sheer stupidity on Hegel's part. Rather, he saw that to understand history in its totality, to see its truth as a whole, one must view it from the perspective of the end of history. Hegel was right in seeing the need for an end-historical standpoint, but wrong in identifying his own philosophy with the absolute standpoint.[20]

In the Biblical eschatological interpretation of history, the end of history has already occured—proleptically—in Jesus of Nazareth. Therefore, the finally valid revelation has taken place in Jesus of Nazareth, since, as Pannenberg's thesis 2 states, revelation happens not at the beginning but at the end of history. But, in difference from Hegel, the future remains open; history goes on; promises have yet to be fulfilled. The occurrence of the end of history within the midst of history happened in the resurrection of Jesus from the dead. But what has happened to him remains outstanding, still unaccomplished, for the rest of us. A radically realistic doctrine of the resurrection as a historical event is essential to Pannenberg's theology of revelation as history. The discussion of this most exciting theme in the last decade of scholarly research will be the subject of Chapter IV.

The resurrection of Jesus, however, cannot be asserted merely as the self-understanding of faith, nor as a demythologizable element in the kerygma of the early church, as card-carrying Bultmannians claim. The Old Testament apocalyptic view of history, with its emergent universalism and expectation of the end of history, is an indispensable presupposition of the event of the resurrection of Jesus. With Pannenberg, and a growing number of other theologians, the Old Testament has recovered its place of central significance for Christian theology, and is ridding itself of the museumlike quality that it acquired in the regnant period of the history of religions school. In our chapter on the relevance of the Old Testament for Christian faith (Chapter V), we shall see that the same tensions which show up everywhere in theology today between a *Heilsgeschichte* and an existentialist interpretation of Biblical revelation have projected themselves also onto the ground of Old Testament theology. Here, too, Pannenberg and his friends are looking for solutions of a holistic kind, particularly by going beyond the limited but promising start made by Gerhard von Rad.[21]

CHAPTER II

Theology and the Historical-Critical Method

THE LEGACY OF LIBERALISM

The historical criticism of the Bible is still regarded by many Christians as a fifth columnist working to destroy loyalty to the faith. Not that historical criticism itself is out of favor with these Christians. Indeed, ever since the Reformation the most conservative Protestants have applied their own criticism of history to demonstrate that the Roman Catholic Church was founded on a series of legends propping up the institutions of papacy, episcopacy, and the sacrifice of the Mass. But when it comes to the Bible they draw the line. They see Biblical criticism as the *enfant terrible* of Protestant scholarship, with a very bad bringing up in humanism, deism, and radical German liberalism.

It has taken the church a long time to accept in principle the historical approach to the Bible. Paul Tillich offers the following characterization of the daring attitude of pioneering Protestant scholars who did not stop short at the Bible in applying their critical methods: "The historical approach to Biblical literature is one of the great events in the history of Christianity and even of religion and human culture. It is one of the elements of which

Protestantism can be proud. It was an expression of Protestant courage when theologians subjected the holy writings of their own church to a critical analysis through the
historical method. It appears that no other religion in
human history exercised such boldness and took upon itself the same risk."[1]

It is an undeniable fact that the historical-critical study
of the Bible is a legacy of Protestant liberalism. Today, the
historical canons of research are applied—of course, in a
more or less mild form—in the teaching of the Bible in
conservative, even traditionally fundamentalist, colleges
and seminaries. The question that soon emerges is whether
the historical method as such can be liberated from its
"accidental" historical connections with liberalism. There
is little doubt that this question is capable of being answered in the affirmative. Liberal and conservative theological positions are equally adjustable to the findings of
historical research. The most convincing evidence of this
is the facility with which Roman Catholic theologians are
finding a new support for the Catholic conception of
dogma in the results of the form-critical approach to the
New Testament.[2] Bultmann's so-called radicalism is not
anathematized but assimilated without doing violence to
Roman Catholic teaching on revelation, tradition, dogma,
and faith. Obviously, this only proves that it is possible,
to a remarkable degree, to free a method from the particular ideological matrix in which it originated. Acceptance of the critical methods of Biblical scholarship in
no way binds one to the "dogmatics" which a particular
theologian wishes to support through his findings. The
historical method is proving to be like a football which
bounces for and against both sides.

One thing has become absolutely clear in modern theology. There is no turning back to a precritical age of

Biblical interpretation. Those who still feel that Biblical criticism is inimical to the Christian faith will sooner or later have to come to terms with the enemy, either by way of peaceful coexistence or by winning him over to their side. After all, the Bible itself gives us the imperative to "discern the spirits." The word "criticism" comes from the Greek *krinein,* meaning to discriminate, to discern, to judge. Powers of discrimination are also required in Biblical interpretation, else the worst absurdities will be derived from the Bible. There is no heresy or foolish idea in the whole history of the church which has not appealed for support to the Bible. And contrary to the wishful thinking of fundamentalists today, the theory of a verbally inspired, inerrant, and infallible Bible—which has been dominant through most of church history—never served as a bulwark against heresy. Most of the heretics were ardent Biblicists of the most literalist kind. Whatever one's doctrine of Scripture, the critical task is unavoidable.

Not all ages have looked at the Bible from the perspectives of *historical* criticism. In the ancient church, criticism took the form of allegorical exegesis; Luther broke through to an elementary form of grammatical-historical exegesis, but controlled it very much by a Christological intention; Protestant orthodoxy lapsed into a harmonistic approach, bringing Bible passages into line with dogmatic truths; and the period of rationalism, notorious for its lack of historical sensitivity, searched the Scriptures for illustrations of universal laws of human behavior under the aegis of a rationalist dogma of a fixed human nature, always and everywhere the same. David Hume, in his *Enquiry Concerning Human Understanding,* clearly represents the conviction of the Enlightenment: "Mankind are so much the same, in all times and places, that *history informs us of nothing new* or strange in this particular. Its chief use is only to discover the constant and universal principles of human nature."[3] It was not until the nineteenth century that the historical perspective claimed total independence from dogmatic or metaphysical assumptions which imposed an a priori web of interpretation upon the facts of history. Facts for their own sake became the concern of the historian. Leopold von Ranke, the great German historian, formulated the ideal of the historian—to discover what actually happened. When historical principles were then applied to the Bible, it turned out that "what actually happened" appeared very much different from what the tradition for several millenniums had taught. Ongoing criticism opened a wide gap between the traditional and the modern historical outlooks on the Bible.

How should theology respond to that gap? Several answers are possible: outright *rejection* of the historical-critical method, bold negotiation for peaceful *coexistence,* or painstaking *integration* of the historical and dogmatic disciplines.

There are still lingering efforts to rule out the critical-historical method. In rebuttal to Gerhard Ebeling's essay "The Significance of the Critical Historical Method for Church and Theology in Protestantism,"[4] a German pietist, Erwin Reisner, has roundly condemned the historical method as the invention of the blind and haughty unredeemed reason of fallen mankind.[5] It elevates its own autonomous reason at the expense of the sovereign revelation of God in the Bible. The questions and criteria of historical judgment infect a pure theology of the Word of God. Although God revealed himself in the historical figure of a man, Jesus of Nazareth, this does not justify the use of the historical mode of inquiry. The Bible brings reason itself under judgment. The only legitimate type of criticism in which reason can indulge is self-criticism. The revelation of God must be taken on its own terms, or not at all. Theology has no business adopting the method of unbelievers, or accommodating itself to its results.

The way of outright rejection by people like Reisner is understandable in view of the highly ambiguous career of the historical approach in Biblical scholarship. When bound to a closed naturalistic or positivistic world view, it leaves no room for the living God of the Bible. However, there are really no reputable scholars today who propose such a radical and obviously self-refuting solution as that of simple rejection of the historical method. Most see that the historical method has had within itself the power of self-criticism, so that when it has fallen prey to a particular world view, in due time it has freed itself and corrected its mistakes.

EXISTENTIALIST HISTORIOGRAPHY

A fundamental collision between the results of historical criticism and the interests of Christian faith can be avoided by a theory of two kinds of history, or, what amounts to the same thing, two modes of knowledge. An *entente cordiale* can be worked out between the historian and the believer who both have a stake in history. The existentialist concept of history, classically represented in the theology of Rudolf Bultmann, provides us with a convenient bifocal view of historical reality that places historical facts and existential faith out of reach from each other. There can be no conflict between the findings of the historical scientist, however negative, and the concerns of faith. Conflict would presuppose a common point of contact, a shared frontier. Bultmann's response to the warring tensions between the historical-critical treatment of the Bible and faith's regard for it as the Word of God was by radical separation, setting up a neutral zone between them, and having the theologian police it.

The existentialist view of history arose as a response to nineteenth-century positivistic historiography which searched the past for "brute facts," ordered them in casual sequence, and called that history. This history could be reconstructed only by a historical scientist who remained objective, impartial, and disinterested over against his material. As a truly scientific man, the historian must have no ax to grind, no propaganda to make, and no philosophical presuppositions guiding his inquiry. The existentialists realized that there was more to history than that. James Robinson puts it this way: "The nineteenth century saw the reality of the 'historical facts' as consisting largely in names, places, dates, occurrences, sequences, causes, effects —things which fall far short of being the actuality of history, if one understands by history the distinctively human, creative, unique, purposeful, which distinguishes man from nature."[6] History consists of two layers, one of historical facts that can be objectively established, the other of existential meanings that one can perceive only through participation and involvement, through dialogue and personal encounter with history. Existentialists call upon two different German words for history—*Historie* and *Geschichte*—to label the two levels of history. *Historie* is the sum total of historical facts lying "back there" in the past which can be objectively verified; the mode of knowledge appropriate here is impartial investigation and neutral observation. *Geschichte* has to do with phenomena that concern me existentially, that make some demand upon me and call for commitment; the mode of knowledge with exclusive right at this level is existential experience—acknowledgment.

This play upon two different terms for history has been most widely publicized in connection with the new quest of the historical Jesus—our concern in the next chapter. However, these terms also have a bearing on the question of an ontology of history generally. Most scholars today, whether linked with existentialism or not, recognize the need for some kind of distinctions when dealing with historical reality. In historical research there is apparently a theologically neutral level of discovering, examining, and criticizing, by various objective criteria, documents of history and ascertaining from them a body of so-called factual material. But at some point the question of meaning, of interpretation, arises which no historian can escape. His interpretation will be guided by presuppositions which are so much a part of him that he cannot suspend them at will. Existentialist historiography has highlighted this dimension of meaning, the inescapability of presuppositions in interpretation, the historian's involvement with history, the demand for decision and responsible action in relation to the historical texts that impinge upon life. At the same time, however, existentialism has been unable to show how existential meanings arise out of the historical facts to which they are in some way purportedly joined. It is as if the facts in themselves are neutral, meaningless, and dumb, as if interpretations have to be imported from the outside, arbitrarily imposed upon the facts from the value-creating subjectivity of the historian. Sooner or later the thought will occur that since meanings do not arise *from* the facts, they do not need to rest *on* the facts; meanings can stand on their own feet, and facts can be handed over to those who are entertained by archaeological studies.

Nothing has stirred up such a storm in recent theology as Bultmann's call to demythologize the New Testament by way of an existentialist interpretation. What has all the fuss and fury been about? Surely not because Bultmann sees the need to demythologize. Who doesn't? Surely not because an existentialist interpretation is intrinsically opposed to faith. It has proved very fruitful in illuminating the structures of existence and the dynamics of faith. And also not because Bultmann's form-critical insights led him to read the New Testament as kerygma. Which of Bultmann's opponents have not taken over this side of kerygmatic theology, mostly without bothering to thank him? And who would deny that Bultmann's interest in the authenticity of faith keeps him in touch with one of the mainsprings of Reformation theology?

The only profoundly serious objection to Bultmann's theology, in my opinion, is its acceptance of a divorce between history and the kerygma. That this is the source of greatest aggravation is clear from the fact that three major post-Bultmannian theologians have singled out this issue as the one that holds the key to the future of Christian theology. The three theologians—Heinrich Ott, Gerhard Ebeling, and Wolfhart Pannenberg—do not respond to the challenge in the same way; in fact, their proposed solutions give birth to a variety of new oppositions. But they do agree that the *Historie-Geschichte* dichotomy is one that theology cannot tolerate.

Heinrich Ott attacks the problem of Bultmann's dualistic definition of history by destroying one side of the dualism. Bultmann constructed an existentialist view of history upon the ground of the nineteenth-century positivistic historiography which he inherited. Positivistic historiography is wedded to the notion of *bruta facta* that can be discovered and established with a high degree of probability. Bultmann does not deny that such facts exist; only, he cannot get interested in them. So he retreats to another level of historical knowledge, existential knowledge through encounter with history. Ott, adopting a slogan from Nietzsche, denies the concept of a brute fact in positivistic historicism. "There are no such things as facts," he says, ". . . only interpretations exist." With one stroke the dualism has collapsed. There are neither two segregated types of history nor two kinds of historical knowledge. Historical reality appears as "an endless field, an endlessly surging and rolling sea of interpretations."[7] These interpretations are not subjective supplements to objective facts. That is the trap into which Bultmann's dualistic theory of history landed. History encounters us as a meaningful manifestation, and the historian who attempts to abstract "naked facts" out of the total single reality of history is not getting at "what really happened" or at what history really is all about. He is doing a piece of detailed research of a highly fragmented sort, and on a shaky ontological foundation.

Gerhard Ebeling has also set for himself the task of overcoming Bultmann's detachment of the kerygma from its historical ground and content.[8] His initial step in this direction has been to look for the material root of the kerygma in the historical Jesus, despite Bultmann's interdiction on the grounds that this is historically impossible and theologically irrelevant. But it is not yet apparent whether Ebeling will be able to take a second step toward a more comprehensive recovery of the essential historical traditions, including the Old Testament, on which the kerygma rests and which it incorporates. His thought still tends to move within the restricted confines of Bultmann's existentialism.

In Ebeling's great apology for the critical-historical

method, he offers a typically Bultmannian argument in recommending its full adoption by theology. He sees an inner connection between the Reformers' doctrine of justification *sola fide* and the historical method. They are two sides of the same coin. Just as the *sola fide* teaches us that we must live totally without securities of any kind, so also the critical-historical method shatters all possible assurances which faith might be tempted to find in historical facts. The critical-historical method functions as the law in contradistinction to the gospel. The liabilities of this critical method are turned into assets of Christian faith.

Rather than having overcome Bultmann's dualism, Ebeling has so far only modified it. He still remains attached to the existentialist prejudice that faith and history mix like oil and water. So his own independent attempt to go beyond Bultmann by grounding the kerygma in history is short-circuited by the existentialist definition of faith with which he comes at the problem. Faith is viewed as an existential act of decision, affirming the meaning of my personal existence in the present moment. Such a definition makes it difficult to see how faith can be compatible with the historical traditions of the faith rooted in the past.

The Babylonian Captivity of History

Our doubts about Ebeling's success in bridging the yawning gap between history and the kerygma in Bultmann's theology will be reinforced when we discuss his contribution to the current hermeneutical debate. On the other hand, Ebeling has rightly seen that to close this gap, the fatal isolation of the historical discipline from systematic theology must be overcome. He calls for theology to go into the fires of criticism without cringing, and to take up the outlook and the results of historical research into its own approach. This will bring about a new shape of dogmatics never before seen in Protestantism.[9] We might all wish for such a thing! But what about the critical-historical method itself? Is this a fixed magnitude to which systematic theology has only to adjust? Does the historical method itself need to become more self-critical, less dogmatic and ideological? Has it been purged of the naturalistic dogmas which in the past have fixed the norms for what can count as reality in history? Has the historical method been fully redeemed from its Babylonian captivity to the natural sciences in the nineteenth century?

Wolfhart Pannenberg is one theologian who has responded to the challenge to integrate the dogmatic and the historical disciplines, to place dogmatics in dependence on historiography, and historical research at the service of dogmatics. Whether this will result in a new shape of dogmatics remains to be seen. As a preliminary step to accomplish this, however, Pannenberg finds it necessary to free the historical method from its bondage to positivism and naturalism. Systematic theologians in the recent past were scared away from too close an association with historical research because they equated the historical method with a dated and one-sided positivistic view of it. Dialectical and existentialist theologians retreated into the comparative security of traditional dogma (Barth) or existential decision (Bultmann). As long as the historical method was controlled by the world view of positivistic historicism, it is understandable that theologians would become hostile or merely indifferent to it. But such a relationship is not satisfactory in the long run.

The separation between the historical method and the Biblical history of revelation is unacceptable for methodological and theological reasons. Pannenberg argues that if there were a better way of gaining knowledge about a past event, then either the historical method would be useless or that other way would have to be adopted as the right historical method, for the chief purpose of the historical method is to ascertain knowledge about the past, and not —as the existentialists say—to make the believer so uncertain that he lives by faith alone. Theologically, if revelation is history happening, and not something above or alongside of history, then why should not the historical method be the appropriate way of finding out what happened? The full meaning of the incarnation of God implies that this happened in the context of the history of mankind and "not in a *heilsgeschichtlichen* ghetto."[10]

Theology can take the historical method seriously once again if the principles of research are freed from an ideological anthropocentrism which denies absolutely the dimension of transcendence in reality. The principles of research as such do not necessarily presuppose that history is driven by man rather than by God. Of course, there is an anthropocentric element in historical knowledge as in all human knowledge. All historical knowledge depends on the principle of analogy, that is, approaching what is yet unknown on the basis of what is already known. Distant events of the past are knowable only because the historian finds some connection between them and present-day occurrences with which he is familiar. The principle of analogy has to be applied cautiously, however, lest it lead the historian to a simpleminded reduction of the past to the present, preventing him from learning anything really new or different from history. History would be allowed to reflect or illustrate only what he already knows, nothing more. This would be to repeat the rationalist prejudice of David Hume who said that "history informs us of nothing new." The point of the principle of analogy is that by starting with what is familiar and similar, eyes are opened to what is strange, novel, and dissimilar. The historian should press beyond the apparent identities or similarities to the really individual and radically contingent phenomena in historical reality.[11]

Has the historian not all too commonly tried to reduce all phenomena in history to laws in analogy to the natural sciences? Such a view of history seems to be presupposed in Bultmann's statement that the "historical method includes the presupposition that history is a unity in the sense of a closed continuum of effects in which individual events are connected by the succession of cause and effect. . . . This closedness means that the continuum of historical happenings cannot be rent by the interference of supernatural, transcendent powers and that therefore there is no 'miracle' in this sense of the word."[12] Within such a world view, the principle of analogy is likely to be absolutized, leading to a tendency to discover only likenesses, regularities, typical occurrences, and recurrent situations. Theology has no interest in denying these aspects of historical reality, but it is equally committed to a perception of what is special, unique, novel, and unrepeatable.

If an event is reported in the tradition, the fact that there is no immediate analogy between it and our everyday experience of reality is insufficient grounds for denying that it happened. The historian, to be free from dogmatic prejudices, must inquire further, and recognize the limits of the principle of analogy as well as the possibility that he may never have the means for establishing whether the event really happened. On the other hand, Pannenberg maintains, there are times when the critical historian will have to deny that certain alleged events really happened, when he not only finds no adequate historical evidences to assert them, but discovers mythical or legendary analogies to them in other historical documents.[13]

Such a view of the historical method is very similar to the critique of historical reason worked out by Richard R. Niebuhr in his book *Resurrection and Historical Reason*.[14] Both Pannenberg and Niebuhr have forged their understanding of historical criticism in connection with the event of the resurrection. Here we have the acid test whether the principles of historical research can go into the "holy of holies" of Christian faith, or must be left behind while faith prepares itself for a leap to an ahistorical level. Both feel that the chief reason for denying the historicity of the resurrection has been the dogmatistic postulate of the fundamental homogeneity of all events. The absolutization of the principle of analogy will shrink the possibilities of historical knowledge as well as remove the historical basis of faith.

HISTORICAL REASON AND FAITH

If God's revelation to mankind comes *as* history, and if the historical method is our only reliable way of dealing with the past, it would seem to follow that Christian faith is made totally dependent on the results of historical research. If faith claims to be based upon truth and reality, not on opinion and fantasy, historical science seems to offer the only objective canons of discernment. The basis and content of faith then seem to be in the hands of the historian, and faith must, apparently, go begging for its certainty. The critique of historical reason, which theologians like Pannenberg and R. R. Niebuhr propose, seems calculated to secure for theology a high degree of objective probability, but at the high cost of complete subjective uncertainty. The problem is this: If believers are told that the revelatory and salvatory events really did happen, so far as we now can tell by the objective methods of historiography, they will ask, "Who says so?" Then it will immediately become clear that only some historians say so, and ever since the Enlightenment they have been a dwindling minority. Besides that, there seems to be something pseudo about a faith that hangs on the changing opinions of historical authorities, giving assent to their problematic assurances. How should the believer, who himself may not happen to be a great scholar, choose from among the myriad of weird historical hypotheses which professionals claim to have established? Alan Richardson expresses this concern: "It is an occupational idiosyncrasy of professional Biblical scholars to imagine that Christian faith rests upon their ability or inability to solve the historical problems that are raised by it. It does not. It rests upon the testimony of a people."[15]

We are heading into the thickets of the age-old and endlessly debated theme of the relations between reason and faith. Confusions abound and disagreements are generated by the slipperiness of the terms themselves. Is faith itself a way of knowing? Does it include a rational element? Does it have noetic content? Or is it merely an attitude, a relationship, a trust, or a confidence? In scholastic terms, is faith, strictly speaking, only *fiducia,* or does it embrace *notitia* and *assensus* as inherently essential components? The respective roles played by reason and faith in relation to God's historical revelation has become a burning question in modern theology. Wolfhart Pannenberg is boldly trying to reverse the irrationalist trend in theology since Schleiermacher, which derives revelation from the experience of faith rather than from reason's knowledge of history.

Behind modern theology's elevation of the category of faith, one sees the towering influences of Kant, Kierkegaard, and Herrmann. In all of them, reason's hold on the object of faith slipped. Sooner than later it happened that the basis of faith had to be based on faith; the content of faith had to be produced by an act of faith; objective uncertainties were quelled by heroic subjective decisions. When in doubt, take a chance! When the truth claims of faith are placed safely beyond the reach of reason, then faith is free to postulate whatever is subjectively satisfying. When word was published abroad that Christian theology now made statements that reason could neither affirm nor deny by evidences within its reach, statements that have no other supportive basis than the positive givenness of the church, its language, kerygma, or faith, then the fatal consequence that such statements need not be taken seriously was quickly drawn by the generally educated public. When faith builds its statements on itself, with no obligation to square them with reason's grasp of history, how can that faith be distinguished from superstition or illusion? This is the disturbing question that Pannenberg has addressed to modern theology.

The common retort that modern man, after all, is not concerned with the old question of the truth of the faith, rather with its meaning, is a dodge that is as apologetically impotent as it is theologically fatal. Gerhard Ebeling makes the striking observation "that the criterion of the understandability of our preaching is not the believer but the non-believer. For the proclaimed word seeks to effect faith, but does not presuppose faith as a necessary preliminary. The actual situation with the church's proclamation today is, however, that for the most part the believing congregation is made the criterion of whether the preaching is understandable, and thereby faith is made a prerequisite of the hearing of the Word."[16] The question of meaning, of understandability, cannot, however, be settled without referral to the historical events from which the statements of faith arise and which they purport to transmit. This raises the question of truth at a level which implicates historical reason in a radical way, according to Pannenberg and his school.

We are faced with what appears to be a hopeless dilemma. If reason precedes faith, the simple believer is made dependent upon the oscillating opinions of historical scholars; on the other hand, if faith is primary, the suspicion arises that faith projects its own basis and content out of itself. The dilemma can be resolved only if what are called reason and faith are not separable acts, following a chronological or psychological sequence, but are actually coessential dimensions of a total act of a person. A split between reason and faith is as intolerable in the last analysis as the separation between facts and interpretations. Bultmann's idea that faith has to do with kerygmatic significances without vital concern for their foundation in historical facts is based on the neo-Kantian distinction between reality and value. But faith cannot survive for long by holding to cherished values "as if" they were founded on reality.[17] When reason's role is removed from the act of faith, nothing prevents faith from being a blind trust or leap into a dark abyss of illusion.

Paul Althaus, who stands in the great tradition of Erlangen theology, has welcomed the new emphasis of the Pannenberg school on the historicity of the saving events. He also agrees that faith's knowledge of revelation in history presupposes a *fides historica,* a sort of natural, rational, historical knowledge.[18] However, he separates this *fides historica* from a *fides salvifica* (saving faith), so that, in contrast to Pannenberg, he breaks the unity of revelation and history as well as the unity of knowledge. For in Althaus's view, *fides salvifica* alone disposes over the reve-latory side of history, and *fides historica* over the historical side of revelation. On close inspection this results in a "Nestorian" conception of historical revelation, if we may be allowed to transpose the categories of Chalcedonian Christology. Just at this point Pannenberg deviates most drastically from *Heilsgeschichte* theology. It fails to unify saving history and secular history as well as historical knowledge and faith knowledge. Against the kerygmatic theology of existentialism, the *Heilsgeschichte* theologians have carried the burden for the historicity of the saving events. Their best intentions have been hampered, how-ever, by remaining glued to a neo-Kantian last.

The point at which the new theology of revelation pro-posed by Pannenberg seems most vulnerable is its doctrine of the Word. The valid emphasis on the objective hap-penedness of revelation has been set in such extreme antith-esis to the subjectivism of kerygma theology, that now the indispensable place of the kerygma as the mediator of the knowledge of historical revelation tends to be di-minished. Revelation speaks to us, we are told, in the "language of facts." These facts are never isolated data, but are transmitted through a tradition saturated with their inherent meaning. The kerygma and faith do not constitute the meaning of the events nor add to it; rather, they intend only to apprehend and transmit that meaning as faithfully and persuasively as possible. A kerygma that is a mere call to decision (contra Bultmann), and not pri-marily a vehicle for the transmission of the redemptive significance of events that happened in world history, would have nothing to do with the New Testament kerygma.[19] On the other hand, however, a response to God's revelation that bypassed the proclamation of the Word, the prophetic and apostolic interpretation of the salvific events, and the tradition of faith that the Creator Spirit accompanies in his illuminative function, would not be the faith of the New Testament. For faith comes through the kerygma, the preaching of the Word, without which the eyes of men remain blind to the events that God has performed.

No doubt the polemical situation in Germany, tense as it is, contributes to the sharp reaction of the Pannenberg school to the "Word of God" theology that has reigned unchallenged for half a century. When one generation turns to the kerygma and faith, the next might be expected to return to history and reason. The pendulum swings back and forth, and nowhere more conspicuously than in German theology. School after school has hastily and short-windedly constructed its theological position on one principle. The ultimatum "either/or" is more exhilarating than the balanced "both/and." Disciples of these schools languish under the tyranny of a single principle. Yet, in Pannenberg's case, there is evidence already that the position is flexible enough to learn from criticism and shake off extreme and unnecessary emphases. In an exchange with Paul Althaus, it has become clear that his intention is not at all to deprecate the role of the kerygma and the Spirit in bringing a person to faith. Faith is a gift of the Spirit, not a product of reason. But this fact does not affect the *logical* priority of the knowledge of historical revelation. The logical and the psychological aspects of the question have to be distinguished.[20] Reason, in its essential structure, is sufficient to grasp God's revelation in history. Actually, however, man's reason has fallen into an unnatural state. It needs to be restored to its purely natural condition; not supernaturalized, but thoroughly naturalized. Therefore, the aid of the kerygma and the Spirit are factually necessary to drive reason to seek God's revelation in history and to establish thereupon a life of faith trusting in the promises of God.[21]

The functions of the kerygmatic word, the preaching of the church, the liturgies of faith, the dogmas of tradition, will be considered in the chapter on hermeneutics. Here we merely pause to note that any depth analysis of the historical method will ultimately lead into the broadest hermeneutical issues, such as Scripture and tradition, kerygma and dogma, church and Spirit, worship and faith, etc. The hermeneutical role of the historical method cannot be abstracted from the larger philosophical and theological contexts in which a given age applies the method. Today, hermeneutical philosophy has made exegetes self-conscious about their presuppositions; and theologians are bestirred by the multidimensional task of translating the message from one age and culture into a quite new configuration of problems and ideas.

The ultimate criterion of an appropriate hermeneutic is a material one; that is, does the hermeneutical method do justice to the matter to be interpreted? The historical method, as an essential component of hermeneutic, should be the servant, not the master, of the Biblical subject matter. Without doubt, Jesus Christ is the center and crucial content of that subject matter. From a great host of topics in Biblical theology today, we have selected three that place the greatest strain on the historical method and provide the sharpest stimuli to the current hermeneutical debate. The three topics are: the historical Jesus, the historicity of the resurrection, and the relevance of Old Testament history. The whole concatenated series of issues we have discussed so far will be more tightly interwoven as they are applied to these themes of current Biblical study.

CHAPTER III

Our Knowledge of the Historical Jesus

THE HISTORICAL JESUS IN RETROSPECT

The historical-critical method has met its greatest frustration in dealing with Jesus of Nazareth. The field of modern gospel research is strewn with the debris of broken hypotheses that attempt to explain who Jesus was and what he means to us. The question that Jesus addressed to the disciples at Caesarea Philippi, "Who do you say that I am?" still strikes us with its original enigmatic force. Even many who do not count themselves among his devoted followers continue to wrestle with that question, and others who will have nothing to do with the Christian church cling to an image of Jesus that stirs within them a high form of idealism.

The story of the search for the real Jesus of history coincides with the history of modern Protestant theology. The land in which this search has bloomed, withered, and revived time and time again is Germany. Scholars in other nations have participated in this search, but usually as a result of prior stimulation from radical initiatives made by German Biblical theologians. This is even more true today than ever. No one can begin to talk about "the new quest of the historical Jesus" without coming to grips with Rudolf Bultmann's theology. But before we do that, it is well to look back over Bultmann's shoulders to earlier attempts to find out who Jesus really was.

The question about who Jesus "really" was could be posed only with the breakup of Protestant orthodoxy. It had been assumed for centuries that the ecclesiastical creeds had given the final and unalterable answer, and whoever did not believe them could not be saved. The rise of historical thinking, however, undermined unqualified acceptance of the Christological dogma, first, by demonstrating its dependence on Greek philosophical categories, and secondly, by showing that the flesh-and-blood quality of the Jesus of history had evaporated into a Christological system of abstract concepts. The transition from the Jesus of the Gospels to the Christ of the Creeds appeared no longer as unquestionably valid and binding upon later generations of Christians. Suspicion was aroused, first in scholarly circles and then among the educated laity, that Jesus of Nazareth was perhaps the most misunderstood personality of all time, and perhaps least understood by his closest followers. Albert Schweitzer, who wrote the classic history of the old quest of the historical Jesus, showed how the zeal to be freed from the Christological dogma was a necessary concomitant of historical scientific inquiry: "This (Christological) dogma had first to be shattered before men could once more go out in quest of the historical Jesus, before they could even grasp the thought of his existence. That the historic Jesus is something different from the Jesus Christ of the doctrine of the Two Natures seems to us now self-evident. We can, at the present day, scarcely imagine the long agony in which the historical view of the life of Jesus came to birth."[1]

The first thing to underscore, then, is that the new interest in Jesus represented a shift from a dogmatic to a historical perspective. Scholars wanted to know the actual personality of Jesus, not merely what his enthusiastic followers said or believed about him. In retrospect, it seems that the nineteenth-century historians wanted a kind of photographic replica of Jesus which could be had, it was assumed, by wiping away the filmy coatings that later tradition had placed upon him. The research, moreover, had to be conducted by scholars who were willing to bury their own presuppositions. Only then could they get at the real core of historical reality. Many of the leading scholars were especially on the lookout for the manipulations of evidence by the protruding hand of traditional dogmatic Christology. But they were not equally sensitive to the role that their own ideological commitments played in their historical work. They were not as presuppositionless as they thought. Between the lines of the great biographies of Jesus we can read the personal religious viewpoints of their authors.

The nineteenth-century biographers of Jesus were like plastic surgeons making over the face of their patient in their own image, or like an artist who paints himself in the figures he creates. There was, in most cases, unmistakable resemblance between their portrayal of the religion of Jesus and their own personal religious stance. It also happened that the scholar usually found about as much as he was looking for. That is to say, he found out as much about Jesus, allegedly on purely historical grounds, as he needed to prop up his own theology. Nothing can make an onlooker so skeptical of New Testament scholarship as noting the frequency with which there occurs a convenient correspondence between what scholars claim to prove historically and what they need theologically. If a given theologian believes it essential for faith that Jesus understood himself as the Messiah, then it happens, with a regularity that cannot be explained by mere coincidence, that this will be proved beyond doubt with historical arguments. There are, of course, notable exceptions to this pattern. In fact, the pendulum has even swung to the other extreme, namely, when Bultmann regards the lack of historical evidence as a prime requisite for genuine faith and a distinctive mark of a theology that is true to the nature of the kerygma. But these remarks take us ahead of our story.

At the end of the eighteenth century, a professor of Oriental languages at Hamburg, Hermann Samuel Reimarus, began the quest of the historical Jesus. He drove a wedge between Jesus and Christianity and left us with a portrayal of a deistic image of Jesus of natural religion. From then on, a long series of new faces of our Lord was sketched with imaginative variations by the biographers. There was the image of Jesus drawn by Heinrich E. G. Paulus as a morally exemplary man who taught the eternal truths of rational religion. On the other side, the supernaturalistic rationalists, desiring to preserve the ancient dogmas intact, were busy scrambling for historical proofs to buttress traditional belief in prophecies that literally came true and miracles that really happened by outside intervention.

The deadlock between the naturalistic and supernaturalistic approaches to the historical Jesus was broken by the mythological interpretation of David Friedrich Strauss. The historical life of Jesus is scarcely discernible, Strauss argued, beneath the overlay of religious mythology. Strauss was not particularly bothered by this reduction of historical content in the Gospels. As a radical Hegelian, Strauss could offer the reassurance that the essence of Christianity abides in the pure idea of God-manhood which entered historical consciousness with Jesus of Nazareth. Once the idea has been projected into history, it no longer needs the support of the original historical event which occasioned its first expression.

The pictures of Jesus drawn by the radicals like Paulus and Strauss were too extreme for most theologians. Their hypotheses were bitterly contested and repudiated, often too impatiently to retain certain valid insights. (Hence, Strauss's discovery of the role of myth in the New Testament was forced underground until its celebrated reemergence in the theology of Rudolf Bultmann.)[2] There were undoubtedly far more "positive" than "negative" historians working to reconstruct the life of Jesus. They were called "positive" critics because they used the new methods of Biblical criticism to establish the historical foundations of the faith. They tried to combine openness to the new science with fidelity to the old message. One remarkable result of the work of positive criticism was the *kenosis* Christology of the Erlangen School. Basically this was an attempt to fit the new picture of the historical personality of Jesus into the old orthodox Christological framework. The modern stress on the historical character of Jesus, on the thoroughly human image that results from historical analysis, could be justified as an essential implication of the divine *kenosis,* that is, his self-emptying and humiliation (Phil. 2:6-8). However, the syntheses of the kenotic theologians were short-lived; the union of traditional Christology with modern biography seemed artificial and unscientific.

If most of the nineteenth-century historical theologians did not escape the "peril of modernizing Jesus,"[3] making their "lives of Jesus" a vehicle for their own modern religious predilections, in Albert Schweitzer we have a man who returned Jesus to his own time and place in history. The eschatological preaching of Jesus, he said, is basically incompatible with modern notions of religion and morality. Jesus is riveted to the first century. Attempts to contemporize Jesus by deleting the eschatology, as the nineteenth-century biographers did to make him the basis of modern religion, collapse under the rigorous scrutiny of historical research.

By the beginning of the twentieth century, the historical approach to the Jesus of the Gospels was nearing exhaustion. Schweitzer's study was signaling the end of an era. His exposure of the modernizing trends in nineteenth-century historiography gave birth to general skepticism. The mood had shifted from bold confidence and naïve optimism in the earlier period to an unsettling malaise, a sense of frustration. One could point to no sum of assured results, no clear directions; and scholars were falling into opposing camps. The stage was being prepared for a new breakthrough.

CHRISTOLOGY AND HISTORICAL SKEPTICISM

Around 1920, the dialectical theologians capitalized on the prevailing mood of historical skepticism. This skeptical mood was effected mainly by the failure of a century of scholarship to find out who Jesus really was and what he was like. Grave doubts were raised whether the task that the historians had posed for themselves was really possible, or at all relevant. With one great shout the dialectical theologians—Barth, Brunner, Gogarten, Bultmann, and Tillich—disclaimed the historical Jesus. They took comfort in the saying of the apostle Paul, "Though we have known Christ after the flesh (*kata sarka*), yet now we know *him* no more" (II Cor. 5:16). This verse became the Biblical springboard of a theological triumph over the historical approach. The historical Jesus of the modern biographers is not the Jesus Christ whom the Bible presents; he is not the Christ of faith. Bultmann sounded the skeptical note in his book on Jesus: "We can strictly speaking know nothing of the personality of Jesus."[4] In the early twenties, Emil Brunner wrote: "The question whether Jesus ever existed will always hover upon the margin of history as a possibility, in spite of the protest of theologians, and of the liberal theologians in particular. Even the bare fact of the existence of Christ as an historical person is not assured."[5] Hardly less severe is Tillich's judgment that, "seen in the light of its basic intention, the attempt of historical criticism to find the empirical truth about Jesus of Nazareth was a failure. The historical Jesus, namely, the Jesus behind the symbols of his reception as the Christ, not only did not appear but receded farther and farther with every new step."[6] Karl Barth stated his conclusion in his usually explosive manner that the gigantic attempt of nineteenth-century "life of Jesus" research is not theologically worthy of consideration, whether it issues in the mildest conservatism or in the most imaginative hypercriticism; there is no good reason why historical research should go chasing the ghost of a historical Jesus in the vacuum behind the New Testament.[7]

The effort of the dialectical theologians to free Christology from its dependence on the historical and psychological reconstructions of the personality of Jesus had already been anticipated in equally radical form by Søren Kierkegaard and Martin Kähler. Kierkegaard wrestled with Lessing's questions: "Can there be an historical point of departure for a consciousness that is eternal in quality? How can such a point of departure be more than of historical interest? Can eternal salvation be built on historical knowledge?"[8] These were, of course, rhetorical questions. For Kierkegaard's answer was clearly that historical knowledge never yields more than an approximate certainty, and a more or less sort of thing is too fragile a basis for the hope of eternal life. Historical inquiry into the life of Jesus can never produce anything relevant for faith. All that is needed are the words of the witnesses who tell us "that in such and such a year God appeared among us in the humble figure of a servant, that He lived and taught in our community, and finally died." And that, he adds, "would be more than enough."[9] The sheer historicity of Jesus is retained; nothing more is really essential. All that is "more" than that falls on the subjective side of the ledger, on the act of faith affirming the absolute paradox of the incarnation. Whatever Kierkegaard's underlying intention, his writings aroused more interest in the dialectics of existential faith than in the objective ground and content of faith.

Martin Kähler must also receive a large share of the credit or the blame for the separation of Christology from the historical Jesus. His influence upon the form-critical approach to the Gospels, his stress on the kerygmatic intention of the Biblical documents, and his idea that the real Christ is not "the historical Jesus" but the kerygmatic Christ have contributed to a tendency to minimize the historical pole of Christian faith. Kähler himself, however, never played the historical off against the kerygmatic aspects of the Christian message. Rather, he invented the now popular distinction between the two German words for history, *Historie* and *Geschichte*, for the specific purpose of uniting history and kerygma. In the title of his polemical book against the "Life of Jesus" movement of the nineteenth century, Kähler used these two words. He called his book "The so-called *historische* Jesus and the *geschichtliche* biblical Christ."[10] The *historische* Jesus which Kähler repudiated was not the earthly Jesus; it was what we might call the modern *historiographical* Jesus. The *geschichtliche* Christ which he put in its place was not a phantom, not an ideal Christ, but the whole Christ of the Bible, namely, Jesus of Nazareth who lived, preached, died, *and rose again from the dead*—living now in the Word of preaching. The kerygmatic Christ is the Jesus of history under a new mode of reality. Essential for Kähler was the personal continuity between Jesus and the kerygma. This continuity could be known by us only kerygmatically, not historiographically. In this sense the "historical Jesus" had to be rejected. After all, Kähler called this the *so-called* historical Jesus, implying merely the rejection of something less than genuine. He would have been horrified to see his thoughts taken over as a way of justifying the detachment of Christology from the real historical existence of the man Jesus of Nazareth, as the Bible portrays him.

The problem that Kähler's formulation raises for theology is whether a deep interest of faith in the New Testament Jesus can be sustained alongside a disinterest in the modern historiographical Jesus, that is, Jesus insofar as he is the object reconstructed by historical-critical research. Can the knowledge of the Jesus of history which faith requires be transmitted by way of the kerygma alone; or does this way need to be accompanied by the historiographical approach? Kähler was skeptical of the powers of historical research. He derived his confidence from the living word and the testimony of the Holy Spirit. The dialectical theologians shared this type of confidence, and made Kähler's theology a supporting pillar of their own theologies of the kerygmatic word.

THE KERYGMA AND THE HISTORICAL JESUS

Martin Kähler's idea that the Gospels are a kerygmatic witness to the risen Christ, and not biographical reports, has been nearly universally accepted by contemporary theologians. But where does the historical Jesus fit in? Kähler did not separate the kerygma from the historical figure of Jesus. Nor was Jesus the mere presupposition of the early Christian kerygma. He was the basis and content of the kerygma, and therefore also the object of faith. Later kerygma theology that thought to find its ally in Kähler has let the links between Jesus and the kerygma fall apart. The problem of the relation between Jesus and the kerygma has become the crucial question in current New Testament study. A kerygma without Jesus is a verbal vacuum, and Jesus without the kerygma is a meaningless surd. The particular terms in which Bultmann has dealt with Jesus and the kerygma have etched themselves ineffaceably into modern theology, and a built-in ambiguity in his thought has provided the momentum for practically all serious work in the field of New Testament.

Taking off from Kähler's basic insight that the real Christ is the preached Christ, Bultmann states: "The crucified and resurrected Christ encounters us in the Word of preaching, and never in any other way. It would surely be a mistake if one here wanted to inquire back into the historical origin of the preaching, as if this could demonstrate its rightness. That would mean to want to establish faith in the Word of God by historical inquiry. The Word of preaching encounters us here as the Word of God over against which we cannot put the question of legitimation, but it asks us whether or not we will believe it."[11] Faith must rely only on the kerygma, and never be allowed to divert its attention to historical facts or theological doctrines. There is only a short step from these statements to a removal of the earthly life of Jesus, his words and deeds, from the content of the kerygma. Kähler never took this step. That would have been totally contrary to his theology and faith. But many have alleged that Bultmann has taken such a step. Yet it is not at all certain that he has really done so.

In passages that are by no means peripheral to his thought, Bultmann insists that Jesus of Nazareth is essential to the kerygma: "The content of the message (kerygma) is thus an event, a historical fact, the appearance of Jesus of Nazareth, his birth, but at the same time his work, his death, and his resurrection. . . . Christian preaching is the communication of a historical fact, so that its communication is something more than mere communication."[12] Here Bultmann appears not to divorce Jesus from the kerygma, nor to regard him as a mere presupposition of primitive Christian theology, an idea he advanced in his *Theology of the New Testament*. Rather, Jesus is the content of the kerygma.

But in what sense is Jesus the content of the kerygma? According to Bultmann not in the sense of a bygone religious personality, a hero of faith, or model of morality. He is the kerygma's content as an echatological occurrence, as God's saving act of grace for all mankind. The kerygma proclaims the eschatological event. This raises a problem. If the eschatological event is at the same time a historical fact, then what is the meaning of Bultmann's decree that faith is disinterested in what lies behind the kerygma, that we cannot and must not penetrate beneath the kerygma

to the historical Jesus? To the extent that Bultmann ac-
knowledges Jesus as the indispensible content of the kerygma, he must also refer faith to something else than
mere kerygma. He says, "I do not deny that the resurrection kerygma is firmly rooted to the earthly figure of the
crucified Jesus."[13] This means that the kerygma is more
than an address, more than a call to repentance and faith,
to authentic existence. It hinges upon a historical fact, the
sheer facticity of Jesus and his cross. But further than this,
Bultmann apparently will not go.

Why has the kerygma so little historical content in Bultmann's way of thinking? Bultmann realizes that if all the
historical content is eliminated, the kerygma loses its attachment to Jesus and balloons into a celestial myth. On
the other hand, if much of the historical content is retained, then it appears that the kerygma becomes vulnerable to historical research, and faith, contrary to its nature
as an existential act of decision, is bound up with assent
to historical facts. To insure faith's independence of historical research, the cost of the premium is the dismissal
of all historical elements in the kerygma. Bultmann, however, makes a single exception: the bare fact of Jesus' historicity and his death on the cross.

It must be asked by what sort of logic Bultmann can
make any exception to his rule that faith dare not rest
upon historical facts, lest it be exposed to the uncertainties
of historical research, and that it would be contrary to the
kerygma to inquire back into its origin in historical fact?
Having singled out the historicity of Jesus and his cross
as essential to the kerygma, Bultmann has already compro-
mised his rule. Here lurks the glaring inconsistency in
Bultmann's theology. To remove any doubt about this,
let us try again to formulate the matter as sharply as pos-

sible. First, Bultmann states, the kerygma includes Jesus as its essential content; secondly, faith is said to rest solely on the kerygma; thirdly, faith is entirely independent of historical inquiry. Therefore, particular historical facets of Jesus' life must be irrelevant to faith, as is everything subject to historical inquiry. But if this rule is extended consistently, it must result in the elimination of Jesus altogether from the kerygma. For Jesus himself, and not merely details about his life, is open to historical investigation. He is a figure of ancient history in the Near East and the subject of datable and debatable historical documents. He cannot be exempt in any degree from historical research.

How does faith become assured of the historical nucleus of the kerygma? How does the believer today gain certainty of the historicity of Jesus of Nazareth, the sheer fact of his having lived and died on earth? Here is a fact that cannot be irrelevant to the kerygma and Christian faith. Bultmann wishes to retain this fact although his existentialist understanding of the kerygma and faith is ill at ease with the whole notion of historical fact. In Bultmann's thinking neither the kerygma nor faith can vouch for the historical content in the Gospel records about Jesus. Historical facts can be ascertained and established solely by the methods of historical research. This must hold true also for the historical fact of Jesus' existence. This means that, for Bultmann also, the irreducible residuum of history in the kerygma, namely, the historicity of Jesus and his cross, is finally left to its fate in the hands of historical inquiry. In the last analysis, Bultmann cannot escape the charge he frequently levels at other theologians: that they make faith dependent on historical inquiry. To the extent that his kerygma has any factual content at all, Bultmann does the same thing, contrary to his intention to make his faith as a believer independent of his work as a historian.

There are two chief causes of Bultmann's difficulty in stating the positive relationship between Jesus and the kerygma, and between faith and historical research. His concept of the kerygma is determined by the idea of existential self-understanding which has no structural relation to history as a course of events. His commitment to existentialism allows him to talk about the historicity of existence, about the understanding of existence in the kerygma, and of faith in the kerygma as being open to the future, but, in like measure, it prevents him from acknowledging the ontological priority of historical reality, the kerygma's radical interest in what really happened in the Jesus of history, and the nature of faith to look to past fulfillment as well as future possibility. The second is that, in addition to his idea of existential historicity (*Geschichtlichkeit*), he operates with a positivistic view of historical facts, as Heinrich Ott has shown. What really happened, and the historical method to get at that, is still deeply enmeshed in the historicistic picture of history that prevailed in the nineteenth century. The heuristic principles and axioms that define the historical method are likewise prejudiced by the positivistic theory of historical knowledge. Without subjecting these to any theological revision, Bultmann has proceeded to extricate the kerygma and faith from the sphere in which the positivistic view of historical reality and knowledge holds sway. For this reason, faith can have no positive relation to historical research.

In relation to the problem of our knowledge of the historical Jesus, the thesis in our previous chapter seems most amply verified. Existentialism is the reverse side of positivism. It accepts the verdict of positivism that history is meaningless, and flees into the inwardness of the self as the alternate locus of meaning. The kerygma as the vehicle of self-understanding is elevated, and the history of Jesus on which it depends is reduced to a single point. The single point, the facticity of Jesus, is retained—although inconsistently—in order to keep a minimal connection between Jesus and the kerygma.

DIRECTIONS OF THE NEW QUEST

Stern opposition to Bultmann's devaluation of the historical Jesus has existed without interruption ever since he wrote his book, *Jesus and the Word*. This opposition has been expressed in liberal as well as conservative circles of scholarship. Liberalism, of course, needed the historical Jesus. A large measure of its interest in the historical Jesus was motivated by its desire to become free from the dogmatics of traditional orthodoxy. Its secret weapon was the historical Jesus. And when orthodoxy found special support in the theology of the apostle Paul, liberalism was at least consistent, taking the side of Jesus against Paul. But it had never occured to orthodoxy to do a similar thing, namely, to hand the historical Jesus to the liberals. Its dogmatics, though not based on critical-historical research, was committed to the real humanity of Jesus as an inalienable part of its Christological confession. It is not surprising, therefore, that when confronted by a new theology that could, to a large extent, dispense with the history of Jesus, liberal and conservative scholars would close ranks to uphold its relevance. Such scholars have never had to join a new quest of the historical Jesus, because they never really abandoned the old one. They never accepted the verdict of the skeptical wing of the form-critical school that it is impossible to get behind the kerygma to recover the Jesus of history. Especially in British and American scholarship the old quest has lived on, only partially modified by the new thrusts from the continent, namely, the form-critical view of the Gospels and an existentialist interpretation of history.

The beginning of a new quest of the historical Jesus occurred within the Bultmann school. By the publication of his essay "The Problem of the Historical Jesus,"[14] Ernst Käsemann rolled away the stone that blocked the passageway behind the kerygma. That was in 1954. Since then the rest of the leading disciples of Bultmann took off in pursuit of a closer connection betwen the kerygma of the primitive church and the historical Jesus. In 1956, Günther Bornkamm published his monograph *Jesus of Nazareth*. Since then a flood of essays on Jesus have been written by Ernst Fuchs, Gerhard Ebeling, Hans Conzelmann, Willi Marxsen, Herbert Braun, James Robinson, and many others, trying to establish more precisely the sort of continuity that really does and must exist between Jesus and the kerygma.

A common concern of the new questers is to reassert the constitutive significance of Jesus for Christian faith. Reacting against Bultmann's view that the message of Jesus is a presupposition of the theology of the New Testament, not a part of that theology itself, Käsemann says, "Christian faith is here being understood as faith in the exalted Lord, for which the Jesus of history as such is no longer considered of decisive importance."[15] For Käsemann, the Christ of the Easter kerygma must be continuous with the Jesus of history; the meaning of preaching and faith depends on it. First, there is the exegetical fact that all four Gospels took pains to establish the significance of the history of Jesus against a spiritualistic docetism which would substitute a heavenly being in place of the man from Nazareth, and secondly, the Easter faith itself, our faith, would dissolve into mythology without the identity of the earthly Jesus with the risen Christ.

In calling for a new quest, Käsemann had no illusions that the difficulties Bultmann faced were now substantially removed. There are no new sources that greatly change the situation, and Käsemann offers no really new view of the gospel records, nor a more viable method of historical inquiry. In general he follows Bultmann's radicalism. He adopts the principle that only those elements in the tradition about Jesus can be accepted as definitely historically authentic which cannot be explained on the basis of either Judaism or primitive Christian preaching.[16] Consequently, very little that is authentic remains after Käsemann's reconstruction. Yet, Käsemann refuses to yield to an attitude of pessimistic resignation in the face of the historical problem of Jesus. He finds that in Jesus' preaching of the Kingdom (*basileia*), God is drawing near to man in gracious freedom. In his preaching and with his very presence, Jesus brings the freedom of the children of God. At this point we have, supposedly, a point of contact with the Christology of the kerygma.

The scholars who responded to Käsemann's appeal for a renewed effort to grasp the historical Jesus are anxious to avoid the pitfalls in the old quest. They do not wish to fall back into the biographical approach, with its interest in chronology, topography, and psychology. There is no inclination to deny the kerygmatic quality of the New Testament sources or to repudiate the insights of form criticism concerning the development of the gospel traditions. We are assured that the new quest is not being undertaken to look for proofs or to verify the faith by historical science. What then is it all about? It seems that they hope to find certain features in Jesus' own message which disclose his uniqueness, which make him more than merely a Jewish rabbi or eschatological prophet. If Jesus were just one more in a long line of rabbis and prophets, what special relevance would he have for Christian faith?

Günther Bornkamm of Heidelberg is the only Bultmannian who has actually written a book on Jesus of Nazareth.[17] Like Käsemann he felt keenly the deficiency of Bultmann's treatment of the historical Jesus. In Bultmann's theology, he says, "Jesus Christ has become a mere saving fact and has ceased to be a person. He himself has no longer any history."[18] Bultmann lays all the stress upon the meaning of the kerygma rather than on its basis in historical reality. In proposing that research now go behind the resurrection kerygma, Bornkamm admits that he is not in a position to lay bare the facts of history, to give a clean description of "what actually happened." Anyway, that would be beside the point. In the early Christian tradition the earthly Jesus is pictured as the risen Lord, and the risen Lord as the earthly Jesus: "In every layer, therefore, and in each individual part, the tradition is witness of the reality of his history and the reality of his resurrection. Our task, then, is to seek the history *in* the Kerygma of the Gospels, and in this history to seek the Kerygma."[19] Kerygma and history are interpenetrating in the Gospels. Thus, for the sake of the history in the kerygma, the question of the pre-Easter stage of the tradition's content cannot be denied. Both faith and historical research demand that historians try to establish the character of the Jesus who evoked faith from his followers. Despite the fact that the Gospels were written in the light of Easter, and are stamped throughout with the Easter faith of the early church, yet "they bring before our eyes, in very different fashion from what is customary in chronicles and presentations of history, the historical person of Jesus with the utmost vividness."[20]

Ernst Fuchs[21] and Gerhard Ebeling,[22] more than either Käsemann or Bornkamm, have attached their inquiry into the historical Jesus to a specific theological program. Together they have worked out a hermeneutical theory that hinges upon the concepts of language and faith. The key to the continuity between the historical Jesus and the kerygmatic Christ is faith as a word-event. They are not interested in a factual, biographical account of the life of Jesus. Rather, they seek what came to expression in him. Ebeling uses the term *Wortgeschehen* (word event) and Fuchs prefers *Sprachereignis* (language occurrence). For both of them, what uniquely came to expression in Jesus was *faith*. To believe in Jesus means to reenact the decision of faith which Jesus originally made. Faith is not a partial act; it is the whole man in openness to the future, living in relation to other men and sharing in the love of God.

Jesus is called by Ebeling the witness to faith, or the witness of faith. He can also be called the source of faith and the basis of faith. But, he is not the *object* of faith. "Faith in Jesus" as a combination of terms is shorthand for attaining a pure trust in the love of God. Today it is necessary to go behind the Christological ideas of the primitive church to an encounter with Jesus himself. Christology is secondary, the faith *of* Jesus primary. The Christological titles in the New Testament have their origin in the faith of Jesus.

The significant thing in Ebeling's contribution to the new quest is not to be found at the historical-exegetical level. It lies in the sphere of hermeneutics, and also in

Christology. His interest in getting beneath Christology to the immediate faith of Jesus is reminiscent of Wilhelm Herrmann's notion of the "inner life of Jesus." Herrmann also wished to refer the believer to Jesus himself at a level deeper than historical fact or doctrinal formula. He latched on to the idea of Jesus' inner life as an invulnerable datum whose overwhelming power one can experience directly. Herrmann's notion of the "inner life of Jesus" did not prove invulnerable; it was demolished by the onslaughts of historical criticism. In Herrmann's view a basic element of this inner life was Jesus' self-understanding as the Messiah. Since Wilhelm Wrede, a great number of New Testament theologians, especially those under Bultmann's influence, regard Jesus' Messianic utterances as retrojections of the early church into the mouth of Jesus. Will Ebeling's notion of the faith of Jesus stand up any better under the weight of criticism? Against Ebeling, Bultmann has observed that the idea of the faith *of* Jesus is foreign to the New Testament.[23] Moreover, how could it help us to know that Jesus believed, that he was a good Christian? Jesus is called the "pioneer and perfecter of our faith" in the New Testament (Heb. 12:2) but Ebeling turns this to mean that Jesus is the prototype of faith. To be sure, we may postulate that Jesus also had faith in the Father, but is this what uniquely came to expression in him? Not according to the New Testament. Faith had already existed in the Old Testament. A whole cloud of witnesses lived before Jesus' time (Heb., ch. 11). Abraham is called the father of faith; John the Baptist may appropriately be called a witness of faith. But Jesus? He must be much more than that, unless we are prepared to accept a revised version of von Harnack's idea that the essence of Christianity lies in the simple religion of Jesus.

We cannot discuss here all the viewpoints of Bultmann's disciples who are trying to improve on his theology. It should be pointed out, however, that in the process of going beyond their master, they have brought about internal frictions of such gravity that the school is dividing into factions. Ernst Käsemann has written essays critical of Ebeling and Fuchs; Hans Conzelmann has warned that the new quest may once again arouse the appetite for historical proofs of the faith; Bultmann has been anything but impressed by the results of the new quest, seeing them as a return to the fleshpots of liberalism. And Herbert Braun, the most radical of all the Bultmannians, has carried the existentialist interpretation of the New Testament to the bitter end, so that the person and work of Jesus are absorbed into a motif of self-understanding. Jesus is only a symbol of a new existential self-understanding; the gospel has been reduced to existentialist anthropology. He holds that Christology is the variable, and anthropology the constant in the New Testament. James Robinson also tries to establish continuity between Jesus and the kerygma by showing a structural similarity between the existential self-understanding reflected in Jesus' preaching and the church's post-Easter preaching.

Despite all the differences among the disciples of Bultmann, in one respect they approach the question of continuity between Jesus and the kerygma in a similar way. They realize the necessity of continuity, but in trying to establish it they all bypass the resurrection as a historical event. Thus they search for a kerygmatic point of departure in Jesus' faith, in his preaching, his attitude or behavior, his self-understanding, his idea of grace, of God's nearness, and what not. Is this enough on which to base the whole development of the Easter kerygma? Yet, once the question of continuity has been posed as a historical problem, and so long as the event of the resurrection is ruled out from historical consideration, there is no other choice but to search for some clue in Jesus' self-understanding or demeanor from which to derive the core of the kerygma, on which to base its development, or to which any test of the kerygma's legitimacy must be referred. In the next chapter, therefore, we shall have occasion to ask whether the historical problem of the life of Jesus can be posed and answered apart from a historical approach to the resurrection event.

It would be misleading to leave the impression that only the Bultmannians are interested in the new quest. Theologians like Joachim Jeremias, Otto Michel, Oscar Cullmann, and Ethelbert Stauffer have welcomed the new quest as a vindication of their long-standing interest in the historical Jesus. They never bowed to the prohibitions—methodological and theological—which Bultmann had enjoined against going behind the kerygma. In his pamphlet *The Problem of the Historical Jesus,* Joachim Jeremias takes the position that we are demanded both by the nature of the sources and by the kerygma to go back to the historical Jesus. The kerygma affirms the incarnation, the Word made flesh, and invites us to see the revelation concretized in the person of Jesus himself. Moreover, the sources do not impede but enable us to establish the *ipsissima verba* (the very words) of Jesus. The words of Jesus' preaching constitute a call; the kerygma is but the response. The call is the more important. To understand the kerygma, we must first hear the call to which it was the response. The kerygma is far from self-evident or self-authenticating, as Bultmann claims.

Jeremias agrees with the form critics that writing a full-length biography of Jesus is now out of the question. Still,

it is possible to reconstruct with a high degree of probability the exact words of Jesus, as he spoke them in the
Aramaic dialect. When we get back to Jesus' own words,
we discover their incomparable uniqueness, why it was
said, "No man ever spoke like that." He called God
"Abba" and there is no analogy to his use of "Amen."
"It may be maintained that these two characteristic features of the *ipsissima vox* of Jesus contain in a nutshell his
message and his consciousness of authority."[24] The more
analogies to Jesus' message the study of the history of
religions discovers, "the clearer it becomes that there are
no analogies to the message of Jesus."[25] Those who hear
his message hear the Word of God. Hence, the most important task of New Testament scholarship is to bring us
face-to-face with Jesus' own preaching of the gospel that
antedates and lies beneath the proclamation of the early
church.

Underlying Jeremias' historical project is a certain view
of revelation. Jesus' own words are the unique and sole
medium of God's revelation. Not the kerygma of the early
church, not the preaching of the church today, but only
the words of Jesus are the revelation. What is bewildering
for us is that a New Testament scholar can say, "According to the witness of the New Testament, there is no other
revelation of God but the incarnate Word."[26] What about
the Old Testament? "In many and various ways God spoke
of old to our fathers by the prophets." (Heb. 1:1.) And
what about the Gentiles and the Greeks of Rom., ch. 1?
But even more catastrophic than this Jesuological monopoly of revelation is the virtual exclusion of the resurrection
as a structural component of the revelation of God in Jesus
Christ. Only the kerygma *of* Jesus, not the kerygma *about*
Jesus, is the revelation, the whole revelation. In Jeremias'
essay on the historical Jesus, there is not one mention of

the resurrection event as a codeterminant of the revelation. Revelation proceeds up to Golgotha; then and there it ends. After that, there arises the kerygma of the early church as a response to the revealing words of the historical Jesus. "Hence, the historical Jesus and his message are not *one* presupposition among many for the kerygma, but the *sole* presupposition of the kerygma."[27]

It is obvious that Jeremias does not take the resurrection into account as a historian. He has accepted the verdict that the resurrection lies beyond the competence of the historical method. The relation between Jesus and the kerygma is merely one wherein the message of the church reduplicates the preaching of Jesus. This, however, runs contrary to the evidence. The early church did not preach the same sermons that Jesus did. At the center of the kerygma of the church stand the cross and the resurrection. This is not the case with Jesus' own eschatological preaching. He did not include himself in his preaching in the way the church went on to do after Easter and Pentecost. The problem of continuity betwen Jesus and the kerygma arises precisely because of the discontinuity between the message of Jesus and the proclamation of the church. The question that theology faces is whether the necessary continuity can be established by going behind the kerygma in circumvention of the resurrection.

Positions to the right and left of Bultmann have drawn nearer together as they join in reopening the door to the historical Jesus. They can be distinguished by the more or less radical way in which they apply the knife of historical criticism, and the theological uses to which they put their results. They also share widely in the consensus that the event of the resurrection forms no part of the historical problem of the life of Jesus. Their efforts to go beyond

Bultmann to establish a material connection between Jesus and the kerygma bypass the resurrection. Hans Conzelmann has formulated the consensus in an unmistakably clear way: "The resurrection was regarded by the primitive church as an event in time and space. . . . Of course it did not *reflect* on the relation between the historical and the suprahistorical. . . . However, as soon as reflection sets in, . . . it is evident that historical research cannot establish the facticity of the resurrection. It can only establish that men testified they had seen Jesus alive after his death."[28] Then, Conzelmann goes on to say, from the way in which they interpreted the death of Jesus out of their experience, it becomes utterly clear to us "that the resurrection is not an historical event."[29]

This consensus "that the resurrection is not an historical event" is being challenged and shattered by some of the more creative theologians of the present day. Perhaps the most significant turn of events in the last decade of Biblical scholarship is the discovery of the resistibility of the resurrection material to all hypotheses that fail to reckon with its historicity.

CHAPTER IV

The Historical Event of the Resurrection

THE IRONY OF THE FORM-CRITICAL CONSENSUS

The form-critical study of the earliest Christian traditions has established beyond reasonable doubt that faith in the risen Christ is the point of departure and the essential content of the kerygma. Without the Easter faith there would have been no Christian church and the New Testament would not have been written. The belief that God raised Jesus from the dead on the third day is as old as the Christian faith and is now, as ever before, the article by which the church stands or falls. In a day when scholars have very few assured results to report from their critical study of the New Testament, it may be refreshing to know that even the more skeptical historians agree that for primitive Christianity, if not for themselves, the resurrection of Jesus from the dead was a real event in history, the very foundation of faith, and not a mythical idea arising out of the creative imagination of believers.

A rough-and-ready sampling of current scholarly opinion will give some impression of the consensus that prevails on the significance of the resurrection of Jesus in early Christian witness. Ernst Käsemann formulates it in this way: "The Christian message is founded on the Easter faith. . . . Primitive Christianity is obviously of the opinion that the earthly Jesus cannot be understood otherwise than from the far side of Easter."[1] Günther Bornkamm is equally emphatic: "To the original Christian tradition, Jesus is not in the first instance a figure of the past, but rather the risen Lord, present with his will, his power, his word."[2] Hans Conzelmann states that "in the New Testament there is no faith that does not begin *a priori* with the resurrection of Jesus. . . . Jesus' resurrection is regarded as *the* salvation event."[3] Gerhard Ebeling sees the resurrection of Jesus as the point of transition from Jesus himself to the church's proclamation of Jesus as the Christ. Then he says: "It must simply be accepted as a fact that early Christianity saw it (that Jesus is risen) in this way, and the proclamation of the church has from that time gone on repeating that Christian faith stands and falls with the witness to the resurrection of Jesus from the dead."[4] And Willi Marxsen, who has tried to establish that many of the pre-Easter traditions were taken over unchanged into the post-Easter situation, admits that "Easter is the presupposition for the fact that Jesus later became the object of preaching."[5]

All the scholars we have quoted happen to be strongly influenced by Rudolf Bultmann. But on the role of the Easter faith in shaping the earliest traditions of the church there is no visible line of demarcation between scholars for or against Bultmann's New Testament theology. The differences first arise the moment the question is put: But what do *we* make of the New Testament witness to the resurrection of Jesus? This is the hermeneutical question of how we interpret for our own faith and theology and in our own world of thought what the evangelists and apostles handed down to subsequent generations. In spite of the form-critical consensus on the standing of the resurrection of Jesus in primitive Christian faith, modern theology is divided on the question whether the resurrection was a historical event. Here lies the irony in this consensus. The historical-exegetical results, even when they add up to a consensus, have no power to produce a common dogmatic judgment. Non-Biblical factors intervene to deroute the theologian on his way from exegesis to dogmatics, so that—as is not seldom the case today—theologians will make statements which even they will admit run counter to central New Testament affirmations.

A great number of theologians have joined Bultmann's chorus in singing the refrain, "The resurrection itself is not an event of past history."[6] Admittedly for the early Christians, as Conzelmann states, the resurrection was an event in time and space and the appearances of the risen Christ were such that the ordinary physical senses of the witnesses were used to behold him. Bultmann himself is not in doubt about that. But for us moderns, despite Paul's appeal to living eyewitnesses in I Cor., ch. 15, "an historical fact which involves a resurrection from the dead is utterly inconceivable."[7] It would be a gross oversimplification to jump to the conclusion that Bultmann, in denying the *historicity* of the resurrection event, thereby intends to deny the *reality* of Jesus' resurrection as such. This suggests the intriguing possibility of affirming the reality of the resurrection in the kerygmatic word, while denying it as historical fact. But is this really possible? Would not the denial of the resurrection as a historical event seriously call into question the basis from which we could judge it to be real in any significant sense whatsoever? What kind of reality would the resurrection event be if it would lie *wholly* outside the bounds of what we experience as history?

The impotence of the form-critical consensus can be explained by the stranglehold that historicism and existentialism together have had on the process of forming theological statements. Form criticism, unlike the older method of historical criticism, did not seek to establish whether the historical events attested by the kerygma really happened. Instead, form criticism inquired into the kerygmatic motives and the *Sitz im Leben* which shaped the developing traditions of early Christianity. Form criticism analyzed the forms of the tradition in terms of the practical purposes they served, whether kerygmatic, didactic, liturgical, or polemical. Form criticism did not say that the events reported—such as the resurrection of Jesus—did not happen; as a method of analysis, it withheld judgment on the questions of reality and truth.

The methodological reserve of form criticism, however, played into the hands of positivistic historicism and existentialism. These isms were complete dogmatic systems of thought and, as we have shown, by no means mutually exclusive. Positivistic historicism was very happy to decree what could or could not have happened in history, since it approached the New Testament with a naturalistic view of history as an unbroken chain of immanent interconnections of cause and effect. From this historicistic point of view, Bultmann's statement can be understood: "An historical fact which involves a resurrection from the dead is utterly inconceivable." However, the negative verdict of historicism could be endured, it was imagined, if one read the Gospel records not as statements about what really happened, but as expressions of faith. These expressions of faith could now be subjected to an existentialist interpretation, which is notoriously disinterested in knowing what really happened. The Easter narratives could be read as stories that enshrine a new self-understanding of existence. If the resurrection did not really happen as a historical event, it could nevertheless be retained in the symbolic language of faith as expressive of a new existential understanding. The interaction of form criticism, positivistic historicism, and existentialist interpretation resulted in collapsing the *Easter event* into the *Easter faith.*

In summary, we have argued that the form-critical consensus on the resurrection of Jesus has been blocked from achieving positive theological results by the intervention of historicism and existentialism. With an assist from Bultmann's theology, there is occurring in modern theology a repristination of the teaching on the resurrection in nineteenth-century liberalism from Schleiermacher through Wilhelm Herrmann. The hallmark of this teaching is the reduction of the Easter event to the Easter faith. We will now trace this line of thought in representative versions of neoliberal theology today.

The Devaluation of Easter in Neoliberalism

In our previous chapter we have shown why Bultmann will not go behind the kerygma to ground it in the historical Jesus. For him the historical Jesus is the *Christus kata sarka* who need concern us no longer. The kerygma is self-authenticating in the actual moment in which it is now being proclaimed by the church and calling man to decide for a true self-understanding. This idea of the self-sufficiency of the kerygma must also, according to Bultmann, exclude any interest in an Easter event which could serve as the legitimating basis of the kerygma. The intention of the kerygma is supposedly to evoke a new understanding of existence, not to report a historical event.

For Bultmann the essence of Easter faith is to believe in the Christ present in the preaching of the church. This faith does not hinge upon a miraculous event in history additional to Jesus' death on the cross. Indeed, "faith in the resurrection is really the same thing as faith in the saving efficacy of the cross."[8] In answer to the question, What happened on Easter day? we can say that the redemptive event of the cross reached its goal in the faith of the first disciples. The Easter event is the event of faith. The real resurrection was the "rise of faith." It was not an event that happened *to* Jesus, but one that happened to the disciples, who somehow were confronted with the questionability of their own existence and challenged to decide, all evidences to the contrary, for the meaningfulness of existence.

Bultmann's existentialist exegesis gambled on the assumption that the resurrection texts were only intent on being vehicles of a new self-understanding, or expressions of the faith of the community, rather than reports of what God really did to Jesus. The gist of the texts would then be the disciples' relation to Jesus, their faith and understanding, and not God's relation to Jesus, and on that basis his relation to the disciples, to the church, to the world, determining the final future of all those who are still to come. However, there is nothing that more directly contravenes the "intention" of these texts than to read them merely as expressions of a new self-understanding. Where is the evidence that the authors of these texts were primarily interested in expressing their new understanding of existence? No doubt they succeeded in doing this by the way, and it is certainly legitimate for us to inquire into the anthropological content and corollaries of their Christological assertions. But we cannot square with their intention if we divorce the "existential truth" or "kerygmatic significance" from the substantive, historical nucleus of the apostles' resurrection affirmations. For the meaning of the Easter proclamation has its center of gravity not in the faith which receives, but in the event which makes the faith of Easter a possibility in the first place. The resurrection event is God's act of exalting Jesus beyond the nihility of death. Without this event having really occurred, there is no existential core of meaning in the resurrection stories worth talking about. The basis of the church's proclamation would thereby be removed and the content of its faith evacuated of all meaning.

The consequences of an existentialist interpretation of the resurrection kerygma, when pursued to the bitter end, are most unqualifiedly visible in Schubert Ogden's book on Rudolf Bultmann, *Christ Without Myth*. Here the *method* of existentialist interpretation has been expanded into a *philosophy* of existence in which the soteriological basis for the meaningfulness of the resurrection of Christ has been undermined. In the New Testament the salvation of persons is connected with faith in the risen Christ. "If you confess with your lips that Jesus is Lord and believe in your heart that God raised him from the dead, you will be saved." (Rom. 10:9.) The presupposition here is that man is in a predicament, in bondage to sin, death, and the devil, from which he cannot extricate himself by his own decisions or by leaping to a new level of self-understanding. But for Schubert Ogden such a view of man is mythological. Pelagius was right after all. "Man is a genuinely free and responsible being, and therefore his salvation is something that, *coram deo,* he himself has to decide by his understanding of his existence."[9] From this premise about man's condition, Schubert Ogden concludes that the bodily resurrection of Jesus "would be just as relevant to my salvation as an existing self or person as that the carpenter next door just drove a nail in a two-by-four, or that American technicians have at last been successful in recovering a nose cone that had first been placed in orbit around the earth."[10] There is only one further step that can be taken, after the resurrection of Jesus has been deleted from the normative content of the Christian faith. That is to make Jesus Christ himself tangential to the faith. Schubert Ogden does not hesitate to take that step. This existentialist revision of the Christian faith is completed with the novel instruction that "the only final condition for sharing in authentic life that the New Testament lays down is a condition that can be formulated in complete abstraction from the event Jesus of Nazareth and all that it specifically imports. . . . Not only is it *possible* to affirm that authentic existence can be realized apart from faith in Jesus Christ or in the Christian proclamation; it is, in fact, *necessary* that this affirmation be made."[11] Protestant theology, we are told, must carry through its historic calling to combat the heresy of works righteousness by now stressing "that God saves man by grace alone in complete freedom from any saving 'work' of the kind traditionally portrayed in the doctrines of the person and work of Jesus Christ."[12] The historic catholic (and Reformation) teaching that God's act of salvation is wrought by Christ alone is absurdly labeled the "final and most dangerous triumph" of "the heretical doctrine of works-righteousness."[13] Following the theology of the liberal Swiss theologian, Fritz Buri, the New Testament is not only demythologized, not only dehistorized, but also to the last degree dekerygmatized.[14] All that remains is a humanistic philosophy of existence that finally has no need of the New Testament or the resurrection of Jesus Christ. It approaches the New Testament under the lordship of modern man, fully equipped with the knowledge of what could not have happened in history and what alone could have meaning for the modern world.

It is more than strange that the existentialist interpretation of the New Testament feels justified in appealing to the Pauline-Lutheran doctrine of justification through faith alone and its underlying theology of the cross as the reason for dispensing with the historical event of the resurrection of Jesus. In the bizarre exegesis of Ernst Fuchs, the result is reached, for example, that to base faith on the historical event of the resurrection would deny the risk of faith. Faith is always a risk, a decision that always has an *in spite of* element. So Fuchs concludes that the apostles who first proclaimed the kerygma about Jesus "had to believe not because of but in spite of their having seen"[15] the risen Christ. When the thought occurs in the New Testament that the apostles founded their faith on the Easter appearances of Jesus, this was evidence of a lapse into a mere *fides historica* unworthy of the true nature of faith. Here Fuchs repeats Bultmann's chiding of the apostle Paul for trying "to prove the miracle of the resurrection by adducing a list of eye-witnesses." Bultmann calls this "a fatal argument"[16]—fatal to the nature of faith as an existential decision that the believer must make in spite of the total insecurity of its basis in reality. Instead of drawing the existentialists' conclusion that faith is especially heroic when taking into itself the utter groundlessness of its affirmations, the apostle Paul did not shrink from admitting that our faith and our preaching are all in vain "if Christ has not been raised." (I Cor. 15:14.) Paul's mention of a list of witnesses indicates that for him, as well as for the apostolic tradition in general, Jesus' resurrection from the dead was an event quite other than faith *in* him. The Easter event includes the apostles' faith, but cannot be reduced to it. The event that establishes faith is the post-Easter appearance of Jesus of Nazareth, who in his exalted mode of being is nevertheless personally identical with the humble form of his earthly existence. The risen Christ was recognized by the disciples as none other than the crucified Jesus.

When Gerhard Ebeling criticizes Bultmann's theology for failing to grasp the continuity between the kerygma and the historical Jesus, he is rightly underscoring that the earthly Jesus is not optional content for Christian faith. Ebeling is asking to what extent the Christology of the post-Easter kerygma is at least present in nuclear form in the pre-Easter Jesus, and therefore to what extent the Easter faith has its roots in the faith of Jesus himself. Ebeling is not satisfied to have a Christological kerygma that has no explicit foundation in the historical Jesus. However, his eagerness to establish faith on the historical Jesus is accompanied by a reluctance to affirm the resurrection of Jesus as a constitutive element of the basis of faith. For Bultmann the basis of faith lies in the kerygma, not in the life or the resurrection of Jesus; for Ebeling the basis of faith lies in Jesus as the witness of faith. On the question whether the resurrection of Jesus is also an essential part of the foundation of faith, and not merely a symbolic expression of it, Ebeling has made a number of puzzling statements. Many of these statements suggest that Ebeling is reviving the well-known nineteenth-century notion that the historical Jesus, and not the high Christology of the New Testament kerygma, is the real basis of faith.

For Schleiermacher, as well as for Albrecht Ritschl and Wilhelm Herrmann, the resurrection of Jesus is an appendix to the essential faith in Christ. It is but a high Christological idea! Herrmann expressed this clearly with his notion that the resurrection does not belong to the foundation of faith (*der Glaubensgrund*), but is an element of its reflection (*der Glaubensinhalt*). Thus the basis of faith is only the person of the historical Jesus; the resurrection is merely faith's way of expressing its new understanding of him. The Easter event loses its status as a new happening in the history of Jesus. We would ask whether Ebeling is not, on this point, warming over Herrmann's theology? Faith (*fides qua creditur*) and the object of faith (*fides quae creditur*) seem to coalesce in such a way that faith loses its status of being radically dependent upon the risen Lord: "The appearance of Jesus and the coming to faith of the man who is granted the appearance . . . are one and the same thing. . . . It was not a case of a single additional *credendum* (the fact of the resurrection), but of faith itself —and that, too, in relation to Jesus as the source of faith. . . . The faith of the days after Easter knows itself to be *nothing else but the right understanding* of the Jesus of the days before Easter."[17] And again: "It is not in the appearances as such, but in faith, that their witness is grounded."[18] Then Ebeling poses two important questions. First, he asks, what does the basis of faith mean? His answer is that the basis on which faith ultimately relies is "not the isolated and objectified fact of the resurrection, but it is Jesus as the witness of faith in the pregnant sense of the author and finisher of faith."[19] Secondly, he asks, what does resurrection of the dead mean? And he answers, "The best help for understanding this is to abandon any effort to form an image or ideas of it."[20] One could scarcely see in these meanings a maximal interpretation of the resurrection of Jesus. Ebeling's writings generally celebrate the importance of faith, but we miss in them a large vision of the history of salvation on which the hope of faith lives. At least it appears doubtful to us that the kerygma—which Bultmann left suspended in the air—can adequately regain its foundations in history by going *around the resurrection* back to the historical Jesus. For everything that led up to Good Friday can be grasped only on the basis of what happened to Jesus himself on Easter Sunday—the day when not only faith said "Yes" to Jesus but God himself spoke his creative "Yea and Amen" to Jesus by exalting him beyond death.

The historicity of the resurrection is even more clearly dissolved in the subjectivity of believers in Paul van Buren's book *The Secular Meaning of the Gospel.* The curious thing about van Buren's analysis is his sharp refusal of the left-wing Bultmannian treatment of the resurrection, because "it has not done justice to the historical aspect of the Gospel."[21] In particular, he faults Ogden for dispensing with the resurrection and understanding faith apart from Easter. Van Buren promises that he won't make the same mistake. He shares in the form-critical consensus which we mentioned earlier. But how does van Buren understand the Easter event? First we learn what the Easter event is not. It is not to be taken as a "fact," for it cannot be described at all and is not open to historical investigation. In a footnote, he takes issue with I. T. Ramsey, his mentor in the analysis of religious language, who understands the resurrection as "an object of sense," and includes the "fact" of the empty tomb in Easter faith. To this van Buren says, "We fail to understand the logic of this conclusion which endangers our whole understanding of the Gospel of Easter by insisting that it is *also* an assertion concerning a body."[22]

The Secular Meaning of the Gospel has been written for the modern man and by a modern man with certain empirical attitudes. When van Buren's empirical attitudes confront the resurrection story, he draws the conclusion that the "linguistically odd" statement "Jesus is risen" is not an "empirical assertion."[23] The statement is not for that reason meaningless. To get at the meaning of the statement, van Buren applies the new-fashioned method of analyzing the function of sentences within various language fields. We are told that according to this Wittgensteinian method of analysis,[24] one detects the meaning of a statement by determining how it functions. The meaning of a statement is what it does, what job it performs. A nonempirical statement, such as "Jesus is risen," is verified by its influence on the behavior of the man who makes the statement. If Peter had been asked what he means by saying "Jesus is risen," he presumably should have answered: "I have a new perspective on life and now I enjoy the freedom to be for others. For me the meaning of Jesus' resurrection is what a new man I am, which anybody can see for himself." Van Buren puts it still another way. "The validation of Peter's Easter assertion is to be found in the fact that Peter too, according to an old and probably reliable tradition, died on a cross."[25] By this logic of religious language, all sorts of doctrine may be validated equally well by the fanaticism and mad lunacy of those who utter them. Heresy of the wildest kind meets this test of meaning as well as sober apostolic teaching. Indeed, the Christian church has never accused heretics of making *meaningless* statements. It has been all too obvious that heretics have not lacked the courage to die on the cross for their beliefs. The question is whether the teachings are true. The criterion of courage is as little relevant to the truth-value of any statement whether that statement has been made by Peter or St. Hereticus. Nor can the truth-value be reduced to the meaning-value, most particularly when the meaning of a statement is translated into its psychological or ethical corollaries, as van Buren does.

Van Buren's interpretation of the resurrection is a complete disfiguration of the apostolic Easter kerygma. For example, when the apostles proclaimed that *Jesus is Lord* over the world, "they indicated that their perspective covered the totality of life, the world, and history, as well as their understanding of themselves and other men."[26] The resurrection event was nothing else than seeing the historical Jesus and life in general in a new way. The disciples experienced a "discernment situation." Then, on the basis of this Easter experience, the apostles created the story of the Easter event. The Easter faith experience, the believer's subjective perspective or "blik," is moved to the center of the stage, with the Easter event receding into the obscurity of an invisible background.

THE NEW THEOLOGY OF THE RESURRECTION

In diametrical opposition to the devaluation of Easter in modern liberal theology, there has arisen a series of Biblical and dogmatic monographs making significant contributions toward a new theology of the resurrection. As long ago as 1933, Walter Künneth published a book entitled *The Theology of the Resurrection*,[27] in which he stated his conviction that the essential problem of Christology lies in the witness to the resurrection of Jesus and that a new theological direction for today must be achieved by thinking on the basis of the reality of the Lord's resurrection. In 1952, Hans F. von Campenhausen made a historical analysis of the traditions of the Easter events and the empty tomb in *Der Ablauf der Osterereignisse und das leere Grab*, showing that many of the resurrection accounts previously adjudged late and historically unreliable had

gained, at a very early time, a firm standing in the development of the tradition and bear the traits of authentic historical reports. Of course he does not pretend that his
investigations can be a foundation of faith. On the other
hand, these studies can neutralize the type of shallow argumentation that draws negative theological conclusions
from the fact that a given report has been historically dis-
counted as late and "inauthentic."

In the 1950's a number of full-scale studies of the resurrection were forthcoming: Karl Heinrich Rengstorf's *Die
Auferstehung Jesus* (1952), Hans Grass's *Ostergeschehen
und Osterberichte* (1956), Richard Reinhold Niebuhr's
Resurrection and Historical Reason (1957), and Gerhard
Koch's *Die Auferstehung Jesu Christi* (1959). Then more
recently still, two younger German theologians have published major works for which the resurrection of Jesus is
historically and theologically the cornerstone of the entire
theological edifice. We have in mind Wolfhart Pannenberg's *Grundzüge der Christologie* (1964) and Jürgen Moltmann's *Theologie der Hoffnung* (1965). They have built
further upon the solid foundations of research that was so
painstakingly conducted by the aforementioned scholars in
the 1950's. All these scholars, from von Campenhausen to
Moltmann, speak of the resurrection as a historical event,
not only of its existential meaning. For them the unity of
event and meaning is an indispensible condition for making sense of the accounts of the resurrection, both from a
historical and a theological point of view. There is little
excuse for pretending eloquence about the meaning of the
resurrection while holding reservations about whether the
event really happened. The assertion that Jesus was raised
from the dead cannot at the same time be theologically
true and historically false. The double-truth theory proved

to be fallacious during the Middle Ages when theology and philosophy were involved in a frontier dispute; it will scarcely work any better today when theology and history explore the boundaries they hold in common.

The case for a theology of the resurrection advocated by Wolfhart Pannenberg is a unique example in contemporary theology of a creative synthesis of historical exegesis, philosophical anthropology, and Christian dogmatics. The credibility and the preachability of the resurrection of Jesus Christ can scarcely be demonstrated today by any theology that methodologically hinges upon a single principle. Here we can only suggest, in a bare outline, the broad architectonic of Pannenberg's position.

Unlike most of those promoting the new quest of the historical Jesus, Pannenberg does not believe it possible to base the kerygma or faith in Jesus directly upon the claim to authority—implicit or explicit—made by the preresurrection Jesus. The question of the continuity between the Easter kerygma and the historical Jesus, which Käsemann in 1954 raised, cannot be answered unless one grasps the connection between Jesus' own claim to authority and God's vindication of that claim by raising him from the dead. A Christology derived directly from the pre-Easter situation would provide no basis for faith's relation to Jesus. Pannenberg says, "Such christology—and the proclamation based upon it—would be reduced to an empty assertion."[28] On the other hand, Pannenberg agrees with the new questers—against Bultmann—that the Jesus of history himself, and not the Easter proclamation about him, must be the actual starting point of Christology. A theology of the resurrection must not be based on the decision of faith in face of the kerygma alone, but must establish itself squarely upon the earthly Jesus. Neither the resurrection kerygma without the historical Jesus, nor the historical Jesus without the resurrection event can supply the basis on which faith and preaching can stand today. Christology, in beginning with the man Jesus, cannot leap over the actual event of his resurrection without depriving the kerygma of its truth and meaning. Otherwise the kerygma's assertions about Jesus are arbitrary ejaculations of faith, devoid of historical reality, and indistinguishable from superstition.

The resurrection of Jesus and its reception did not happen in a vacuum, as if the witnesses who first saw and proclaimed the risen Jesus had no prior understanding of the meaning of resurrection. Van Buren's statement that "there is nothing in the pre-Easter situation which points toward Easter itself" and that "there is no ground for assuming that the disciples expected anything more to happen" does not square with the facts. In the pre-Easter situation there was, at least among those who shared the apocalyptic expectations in postexilic Judaism, including Jesus and his disciples, a clear eschatological hope for a resurrection of the dead. When the resurrection happened, there already existed the language of hope ready to be used in the proclamation. Pannenberg states: "For the Jewish contemporaries of Jesus, so far as they shared the apocalyptic expectation, the event of the resurrection did not first need to be interpreted, but spoke to them in its own language."[29] They had a good inkling of the *meaning* of the resurrection before it happened.

What, then, would the resurrection mean to those who shared the hope? Pannenberg summarizes this for us in a few propositions. First, the resurrection is a clear sign of the eruption of the end of the world. Secondly, if Jesus was raised, that would mean to a Jew that God has corroborated

Jesus' claim to authority, and in that case Jesus had not committed a blasphemy by setting himself in the place of God. Thirdly, it was on the basis of the resurrection of Jesus from the dead that the post-Easter community identified Jesus with the coming Son of Man. Fourthly, because the end of the world has already broken in through the resurrection of Jesus, God's final self-revelation can be said to have occurred in Jesus of Nazareth. This assertion is tied to Pannenberg's view that in the Bible, God reveals himself as God only from the standpoint of the end of history. This end has been preactualized in the resurrection of Jesus. Fifthly, the resurrection of the crucified Jesus is the motive for the mission to the heathen. Without the resurrection, the Christian movement would have remained a small sect within Judaism. Sixthly, the words of the risen Lord are to be understood as the explication of the significance inherent in the resurrection itself. Therefore, the event is not a mere *brutum factum* subject to ambiguous interpretations. It is united with the word that expresses the meaning inherent in the event—a meaning not imported from the outside. This unambiguous, self-explanatory event is the real basis of faith and preaching.[30]

The expression "resurrection from the dead" is quite clearly a metaphor. To take it literally would be absurd, and would contradict the entire imagery in the New Testament. What this image conveys to us is that just as men arise from sleep in the morning so shall the dead arise from their graves. The analogy of awaking from sleep was used throughout the apocalyptic literature in speaking of the ultimate destiny of those who have died.[31] Those who have used this metaphor have known that their limited manner of speaking by no means grasps the reality of that which will really occur in the resurrection. But they would not have listened to Ebeling's counsel quoted above that "the best help for understanding this is to abandon any effort to form an image or ideas of it." How can preachers, in any case, afford the luxury of the mystic silence? We can only speak by way of images concerning dimensions of reality that go beyond the everyday events and objects of our life. When we keep in mind that we are using picturelike language, we will not fall into the trap of viewing the resurrection of Jesus as a mere resuscitation of a corpse. Following Paul's exposition in I Cor., ch. 15, Pannenberg finds guidelines for our own thinking about the resurrection. For Paul the resurrection means radically new life in a new body, not the return of the same old life in the perishable, fleshly body.[32] The new body is a *sōma pneumatikos,* a spiritual body. Yet, there is a continuity between the old and the new body; it is precisely the earthly, mortal body which is transformed into a new mode of existence, an immortal spiritual body. The transformation is radical; all is new, yet there is an essential continuity between the crucified body of Jesus and his risen form of life.

It would now seem imperative to show that the conception of a resurrection from the dead has relevance for today, that it is not merely an outmoded fragment of an obsolete myth in the environment of late Judaism. Pannenberg believes it possible, and indeed necessary, to show that the main features of the apocalyptic eschatology, such as the resurrection of the dead, the end of the world and the final judgment, can be true for us today. If this is not possible, the continuity between present-day Christianity and the primitive Christian faith has been broken; the foundation of authentic Christian faith has been shattered. "Only if the expectation of the future general resurrection of all men from death, whether for life or for judgment, makes sense in itself, only if it also expresses the truth for

us, will it then be meaningful to put the question of Jesus'
resurrection as a question of historical importance."[33] At
this point the contributions of philosophical anthropology
become significant. A phenomenology of human existence
will disclose that man is by nature one who hopes for fulfillment beyond death.[34] It is essential to man's self-understanding as man to seek his final destination beyond the
confines of this mortal life.

If the phenomenology of existence reveals that hope is a
structural element of the life of man, who knows himself
to be a being unto death, then the question of life beyond
death is unavoidable to man as man. This does not mean
that some men will not even succeed in quashing that
existential question. It does mean that it belongs to man's
humanity to raise the question whether there is anything
to hope for beyond death. "If death is the end, all hope for
a future fulfillment of existence seems to be foolish. For,
how dumb it is to long for a future . . . which only brings
the grave closer."[35] The hope of man for a future fulfillment has been expressed in the history of philosophy by the
idea of the immortality of the soul. Pannenberg does not
believe that this expression can be used today in view of
our modern knowledge of the psychosomatic unity of man.
The idea of a resurrection from the dead better expresses
that it is the whole man, not merely his soul detached from
the body, who is the subject of the fulfillment beyond
death.[36]

Before Pannenberg even raised the historical question of
Jesus' resurrection, he found it necessary to examine the
presuppositions under which the historical question could
be taken seriously. The first presupposition was the prior
expectation of the resurrection from the dead in late Jewish apocalypticism, without which a resurrection event
would not have been grasped. The second is hope for ful-

fillment beyond death as a structural element of human existence—to be disclosed phenomenologically—without which the witness to the resurrection of Jesus would not be heard as existentially, that is, soteriologically, significant. "If one assumes that the dead cannot rise, that an event of this type can never happen, the result will be such a strong prejudice against the truth of the early Christian message of Jesus' resurrection, that the more precise quality of the particular testimonies will not be taken into consideration in forming a general judgment."[37]

Pannenberg is right! Prejudices do have to be cleared away before the historian will possess the frame of mind to treat the historical evidences of the resurrection as "evidence." Perhaps historians have never acted more unprofessionally than when dealing with the New Testament testimonies to the resurrection of Jesus Christ. This happens when inflexible assumptions about the nature of man and of the world prejudge that such a thing could never have happened. The historical problem of the resurrection of Jesus thus has two sides, the historical testimonies themselves and the whole complex process which historians use in forming historical judgments about them.

THE HISTORICAL PROBLEM OF THE RESURRECTION

When the historian raises the question of the historicity of the resurrection of Jesus, he will have to concern himself both with the nature of the reports and with what he himself intends by the concept of history. Only then can he meaningfully answer whether the resurrection is a historical event. We have already pointed out that today there exists a form-critical consensus that in the Easter accounts the resurrection of Jesus was considered, however unreflectively, a real event in time and space that did not originate first in the faith consciousness of the community. It was an extramental reality. Yet there are many for whom the form-critical consensus has no theological relevance, who doubt or deny that the resurrection was really a historical event.

The new theology of the resurrection operates with a concept of history that has been formed, at least in part, by taking into account the kinds of events that the Bible reports as decisive for the history of mankind. The resurrection is such an event. Richard Reinhold Niebuhr advanced the thesis that the concept of history and the principles of historical method have to be forged in the light of the resurrection tradition. "It is because theologians so often try to endow a Christian faith born of the resurrection of Christ with a heterogeneous epistemology that their treatment of the final chapters of the Gospels is so pale. . . . The resurrection event, as it is reflected in the New Testament, epitomizes the historical event itself while the resurrection tradition illuminates the nature of historical thought."[38] It would be methodologically inappropriate for modern historians to challenge the resurrection texts with their ready-made concept of history, without exposing themselves to the demand of the texts that they criticize, and if necessary revise, their idea of historical reality. The historian and his preconceived ideas about history must be made as vulnerable as the documents he investigates.

Jürgen Moltmann has shown how the modern preunderstanding of what is historically possible stands in direct conflict with the Biblical view of historical possibility.[39] In the Bible, historical reality is open to the activity of God. Modern ideas of historical possibility and probability have been developed in complete indifference to the Biblical picture of God as the subject of history. If only that is historical which is "humanly possible" and in principle repeatable and calculable in human experience, then it is obvious that the resurrection of Jesus is both impossible and meaningless. But the procedure can be reversed. It is possible to define history in the light of the reality of Jesus' resurrection. "Therefore," says Moltmann, "the historical question of the reality of Jesus' resurrection also turns back upon the inquiring historian and calls into question the basic experience of history from which he makes his historical inquiry. The historical question of the historicity of the resurrection of Christ thereby eventually results in the questionability of his historical dealing with history."[40] The point of our second chapter on "Theology and the Historical-Critical Method" was to indicate the need for a new concept of history which is freed from a mechanistic and positivistic definition of the nature of history. Short of this, theology will be forced to speak of the resurrection as "unhistorical," as the existentialists do, suggesting the easy inference that it didn't happen, or amounted only to an internal movement of the heart and conscience of believers. If theology abandons the concept of the historical in connection with the resurrection, then not only is the objectivity of the resurrection event in doubt, but also the resurrection loses its relevance for all of history itself and for our knowledge of history. It becomes merely a private affair of believers and their individual decisions.

The decision as to whether or not the resurrection of Jesus is a historical event cannot be made on the basis of a general consideration of the nature of historical reality. The latter can at best only prepare the way for a careful analysis of the Easter traditions handed down by the early church. Such an analysis must take the measure of the two strands of tradition, one dealing with the appearances of the risen Lord, the other with the discovery of the empty tomb. We cannot here summarize the detailed results of modern scholarship regarding these traditions. This has been done most excellently in English by Hugh Anderson in his recent book *Jesus and Christian Origins*.[41] It can, however, be stated that in general the mood of leading historians today is one which is more open to the historical reliability of the resurrection testimonies. Even the tradition of the empty tomb cannot be so quickly dismissed as purely legendary, as having no historical core. The stories of the Easter appearances of Jesus, however, are primary and least evidently retouched by legendary accretions.

When one reads the modern historical investigations of the Easter traditions, whether conducted by the negative or the positive critics, he will scarcely be tempted to rest his faith upon their results. Of course, the knowledge gained from this historical study will not be irrelevant to faith, for it can serve to remove false hinderances to an appropriate reading of the Gospels. When the way to the Easter message is blocked by prejudices, it is not irrelevant to apply an anticriticism to overcome them. Yet, neither historical study nor systematic reflection (philosophical or theological) can dispose of the dimension of faith and personal experience in one's response to the Easter event. This response is enabled by the preaching of the kerygma within the context of the church's sacramental celebration of the real presence of Christ. In the works of Gerhard Koch, Walter Künneth, and Hans Grass, the sacramental dimension of the Easter faith is brought out. The understanding of the Easter texts will necessarily be conditioned by whether one celebrates today the Lord's presence within the community of his body. The purely historical observation that it can be ascertained with a high degree of probability that the resurrection accounts reported an actual historical occurrence is insufficient to provide faith with its present basis. In the last analysis, the historian's decision whether the resurrection really happened will provide some commentary on whether he shares in the present experience of the church as it worships Jesus as the living Lord. The historical probing can provide a safeguard against the trend to turn faith in upon itself, and be a positive sign to the church that it does not worship an object of its own creation. Thus, historical research upon the Easter proclamation will be united with a theology of worship.

In a later chapter on hermeneutics, we will deal with worship as an integral factor in the transmission of the gospel, as a medium of the self-contemporization of the risen Christ. For I simply cannot believe that a historian's judgment would lean weightly in favor of the historicity of the resurrection unless, *inter alia,* he were motivated to appreciate the historical basis of his actual faith knowledge of the risen, present Christ. I agree with Alan Richardson, who says: "Apart from faith in the divine revelation through the biblical history, such as will enable us to declare with conviction that Christ is risen indeed, the judgment that the resurrection of Jesus is an historical event is unlikely to be made, since the rational motive for making it will be absent."[42] On the other hand, when Christian theologians do make this judgment, they ought not to abdicate the field of historical reality and research in making it. Otherwise the ironical conclusion must be drawn that faith closes rather than opens the eyes of reason to the reality of history in which God has revealed himself. Historical reality that is qualified by the resurrection of Jesus as its aim and meaning does not elude the methods of historical reason; yet reason needs faith as the dynamic of its vision. What reason sees is seen by reason, but *that* reason sees what it sees is made factually possible by faith. In the case of the resurrection of Jesus, what reason sees, albeit not without faith, is not less than historical. Faith and history are not essentially opposed to each other. In Jesus Christ they intersect.

CHAPTER V

Heilsgeschichte and the Old Testament

THE CONTROVERSY PAST AND PRESENT

All the problems we have discussed so far converge upon the Old Testament. The idea of history as the medium of revelation has its strongest protagonists in the field of Old Testament scholarship. Despite the clarity with which the New Testament expresses the same idea in the incarnation, the *Word made flesh,* the dominant school in modern New Testament scholarship, namely, the Bultmannian school of existentialist interpretation, has reduced the historical foundations of the Christian faith to a pitiably few number of points in the total course of Biblical history. In this school the idea of a Biblical *Heilsgeschichte* (history of salvation) has been rejected as a nineteenth-century mixture of philosophy of history with naïve objectifications of faith. In the meantime, however, it has become obvious to many scholars that the existentialists' rejection of the idea of *Heilsgeschichte* amounts to more than a mere dissolution of a particular nineteenth-century school of thought.[1] It includes a theological indifference to the concrete historical traditions of the Old Testament witness to God's acts in the midst of Israel's earthly pilgrimage. Modern existentialist theology, as relevant as its insights have been into the nature of human existence, has come to grief on its treatment of the Old Testament.

Persistent probing into the question of the continuity between the historical Jesus and the kerygmatic Christ has also opened the door from the side of New Testament scholarship into the Old Testament. No special pleading on the part of Old Testament scholars is needed to demonstrate the absolute indispensability of the Old Testament in identifying Jesus as the Messiah and believing in him as the risen Lord. The quest of the historical Jesus would be a pure abstraction if Jesus' attachment to the Old Testament were not with equal seriousness investigated. Nor could Jesus' resurrection be considered as more than a freakish occurrence unless its meaning were grasped against the background of the expectation of the resurrection of the dead in apocalyptic eschatology. In short, the question of the meaning of the events attested to in the New Testament cannot be answered by confronting the reports *directly* with our existential queries, for the present and future meanings of those events are embedded deeply in the past dealings of God with his covenant people, Israel. Just as the meaning of the early church's kerygma hinges upon what God actually was doing in the life, death, and resurrection of Jesus of Nazareth, so also the meaning of God's act in Christ turns upon the prior actions of God with Israel. Our concern for Jesus Christ drives us into the Old Testament. For Jesus is the fulfillment of the Old Testament promises. The fulfiller is inseparable from that of which he is the fulfillment.

But it has not always been so obvious that the Old Testament possesses canonical relevance for the Christian church. Even today the Old Testament is a much disputed book, not only among those who stand outside the church, but among many within it who think they can have Christ without the Old Testament. The church has engaged in a long and at times fierce struggle to show that those who want a Christ without the Old Testament possess a false Christ. In our own century the "German Christians," with rigorous consistency, expressed their anti-Semitism by trying to purify Christianity of the Old Testament. In his *Myth of the Twentieth Century,* Alfred Rosenberg proposed that the religion of the pure Aryan race would have to rid itself once and for all of the book of the Jews with its inferior notions of a tyrannical God. In this struggle against the Nazi-Christian attack on the Old Testament, the church rediscovered the power of the word of the living God speaking through the Scriptures of the Old Covenant.

The controversy over the Old Testament reaches back into the second century when Marcion wrote a book to prove that the gospel and the Old Testament contradict each other. He conceived of two Gods, the God of the Jews and the God of the Christians. The Old Testament God was the author of law, vengeful and bloodthirsty; the God of the gospel was the author of love, abrogating the law and the prophets, and overcoming the evil works of the Creator God. Every association of Christianity with Judaism had to be severed. Orthodoxy responded to Marcion's attempt to separate the two Testaments by welding them together in a doctrinal system that blurred basic distinctions. It used the devices of allegorical exegesis. From the extreme of radical separation it seems that ecclesiastical orthodoxy swerved in the opposite direction of an uncritical harmonization. Both ways represent a loss of the Old Testament to the Christian church. For what is the practical difference between rejecting the Old Testament outright, on the one hand, and reading into it everything that one has learned from the New Testament, on the other hand? The particular message of the Old Testament ceases to be heard in either case.

With the rise of modern historical criticism a great gulf became fixed between the Old and New Testaments. Again, voices could be heard within the church urging the removal or de-emphasis of the Old Testament. Shades of Marcionism returned in Adolf von Harnack's book on Marcion. "The rejection of the Old Testament in the second century was an error which the great church rightly opposed; holding on to it in the sixteenth century was a destiny which the Reformation was not able to escape; but for Protestantism to preserve it since the nineteenth century as a canonical document is the result of a religious and ecclesiastical paralysis. . . . To clear the table and to honor the truth in our confession and instruction, that is the great feat required of Protestantism today—almost too late."[2] The church is asked by Harnack to admit that the Old Testament forms no essential part of her faith and life. According to Harnack, if Protestantism had not suffered from a certain paralysis in the nineteenth century, it would have responded more resolutely to Schleiermacher's recommendation to let the New Testament stand by itself, which alone purely expresses the pious self-consciousness of Christians, or at best to add the Old Testament books to the New Testament as an appendix. The Old Testament did not, for Schleiermacher, share the same dignity and normative status as the New; it did not possess the same degree of inspiration. The church has preserved the Old Testament because of obvious historical connections, but this should not now prevent us from permitting "its gradual retirement into the background."[3]

Similar, if not identical, statements on the relation of the Old Testament to the Christian faith can be heard at the present time. Perhaps no one is openly calling for the removal of the Old Testament from the canonical Scriptures; yet Schleiermacher's view that the Old Testament is only historical background, to be studied as a literary aid in understanding the New, lingers on in current existentialist-hermeneutical theology. In this theology the Old Testament is prolegomenon to the Christian faith; it may be a revelation of the preunderstanding of faith, that is, of man under the law, of inauthentic existence. But the Old Testament is not a document of divine revelation to the Christian church. It is not, like the New Testament, a vehicle of God's living Word to the church and mankind today. Fortunately, those who hold this view are not among the leaders in Old Testament scholarship today. As a recent debate between Gerhard von Rad and Hans Conzelmann brought out,[4] the Old Testament is often made the target of a depreciatory attitude on the part of those who approach it with dogmatic prejudgments about what the Old Testament *must* say, and who are too frozen to their pet prejudices to listen to what it really *does* say. Not least among the offenders are New Testament scholars who have taken their cue from Rudolf Bultmann on "The Significance of the Old Testament for the Christian Faith,"[5] and dogmatic theologians who have allowed Luther's dialectic of law and gospel to break into two separate pieces, the Law representing the Old Testament and the Gospel the New Testament. To apply Luther's formula of law and gospel as a definition of the relation between the Old and New Testaments may have been suggested by certain statements Luther himself made, for example, in the preface to his translation of the New Testament,[6] but the book by Heinrich Bornkamm on *Luther and the Old Testament* shows that, for Luther, this dialectic of law and gospel did not occur merely between the two Testaments, but also within each of them.[7] And, in any case, Old Testament scholarship today has demonstrated how questionable such a formula is in view of the extent the themes of God's love and grace come to expression in the Old Covenant. The law itself is a gift of the grace of God.

TWO VERSIONS OF ISRAEL'S HISTORY

A chorus of voices in the field of Old Testament studies has been raised against traditional schemes of interpretation which muzzle the Old Testament. The most fruitful trend recently has been the patient willingness among scholars to let the Old Testament speak for itself and in its own terms, *before* the final hermeneutical question is put: What does it all mean for us today? The upshot has been a new listening to the Old Testament and a reluctance to write off whatever does not fit our prior schemes of interpretation. Indeed, the force of the Old Testament witness to God's involvement in Israel's history has in many instances brought about a revision of the conceptual schemes which theologians have operated with in classifying, arranging, and evaluating the various sections of Israel's historical and prophetic traditions. The leader in this direction, widely recognized as the world's most important Old Testament theologian, is Gerhard von Rad of Heidelberg University. The publication of his two-volume work, *Theology of the Old Testament,* has triggered a chain reaction of responses, both pro and con, from colleagues in his own field of specialization, as well as from theologians in other fields. Somewhat unexpectedly, the Old Testament has become a "new frontier" in theology.

James M. Robinson has advanced the intriguing thesis that in each generation a particular theological discipline is elevated to the center of theology by virtue of its impact on the cultural environment. Before World War I, Adolf von Harnack made church history such a discipline; after World War I, Karl Barth moved dogmatics to the center of the stage; since World War II, Rudolf Bultmann unquestionably won the position of preeminence for New Testament research. Now, Robinson suggests, "there are indications that Old Testament scholarship could move beyond its departmental confines into such a central theological position in the coming generation."[8] Whether it will do so, Robinson adds, will depend on whether Old Testament scholarship "can relate itself significantly to broader cultural or philosophical currents of the day, in terms of which the Old Testament position could be expressed in the other theological departments and even outside of theology proper."[9] Robinson believes that Heidegger's philosophy may provide the assistance that Old Testament scholarship needs. "Hence one may say that Heidegger has in principle (though not in practice) provided the avenue through which Old Testament research may move beyond the confines of its discipline into a central role in theological and philosophical discussion in our day. What is now needed is for Biblical scholarship to make use of this opening."[10] We have our doubts whether Heidegger's philosophy is conducive to perform such a service, but we would concur with Robinson's point that philosophy can and must play such a role in building bridges between theology and its surrounding cultural environment. The use to which theologians have thus far put Heidegger's philosophy does not arouse much hope that it can do justice to the historical dimensions of the Biblical revelation.

The decision whether the Old Testament can be the point of departure for a comprehensive systematic theology of history, as the Pannenberg circle is presently attempting, stands or falls with the reconciliation of history and faith within the sphere of Old Testament theology. Gerhard von Rad posed the problem in its acutest form when he contrasted two very different versions of Israel's history.[11] First, there is the picture that Israel herself has drawn of her own history. Her confessional description of her own origins and experiences in history is presented as a *Heilsgeschichte,* as a redemptive history of God's actions. Secondly, there is the picture of Israel's history drawn by modern historiographers who apply rigorously the methods of historical science—without a God hypothesis. Here Israel's experience is depicted without taking into account the premises of revelation or faith that Israel wove into her own confessional traditions. If theology is confronted by these two versions of history, is there some way of uniting them, and if not, which one is normative for the church and its proclamation today? A number of clearly different answers are being offered to this question.

Gerhard von Rad is painfully aware of the collision between Israel's witness to her own history and the modern historical reconstructions of what "really happened." We can dispense with neither one, von Rad thinks, but in presenting a "Theology of the Old Testament" the theologian's task is to set forth the history *as* Israel remembered it and passed it on, and not to substitute for it the modern reconstructions. The discrepancy between Israel's kerygmatic portrayal of the succession of historical events in which God's will and word were operative, and the results of modern historical research, which either denies that such events happened or places quite other interpretations upon them, is felt by many to be left unresolved by von Rad. Two clearly distinguishable groups of scholars have come forward with definite proposals on how to resolve the dualism implied in von Rad's position. One group stands in sharp opposition to von Rad, most vocal of whom are Franz Hesse and Friedrich Baumgärtel. Another group, chiefly disciples of von Rad, sees the need to press on beyond him toward a basic theological and methodological resolution of the two representations of Israel's history.

Franz Hesse agrees with von Rad that there is a wide gulf between our present-day knowledge of Israel's actual history and Israel's own conception of what happened in her past. However, facing the same fork in the road, he goes the other way. Not Israel's kerygmatic view of her history, but the real history itself as we now know it to have transpired is the true object of interest to Christian theology. Hesse does not deny that there is a *Heilsgeschichte;* God has revealed himself in history, but not the way Israel imagined. The problem for Hesse is that Israel built a whole theology of history in the air. Modern historical research denies, or at least has no way of confirming, the historicity of those mighty acts of God which Israel celebrated in her kerygmatic traditions. What should be binding to Christian theologians today, and what should be preached from the pulpit, is the historical reality in, with, and under which God revealed himself to Israel. Our faith lives not from Israel's *witness* to what happened; rather, it lives from the events themselves, which appear quite different to us than to Israel. Should we have to choose between kerygma and historical reality,[12] our decision must be against the kerygma. Why? Because Israel's kerygma was based on "facts" that never happened.[13]

Friedrich Baumgärtel offers a somewhat different criticism of von Rad's presentation of Old Testament *Heilsgeschichte.* For him neither of the two versions of history possesses theological relevance. Neither the objective historical occurrences nor Israel's interpretation of history can have significance for the Christian faith. The problem is that the whole "Old Testament is a witness out of a non-Christian religion."[14] More clearly: "From the perspective of our contemporary thinking about the hermeneutical question the fact cannot be eliminated that the Old Testament is a witness from a religion outside the gospel and therefore from a religion strange to us. Viewed historically, it has another place than the Christian religion."[15] One can, indeed, understand the Old Testament Word "in terms of the history of religion, or the history of piety, but not theologically; it remains a strange word from a strange religion, without power, which can only be objectively considered, but it does not meet us."[16] According to Baumgärtel, von Rad's error lies in assuming that Israel's witness to God's actions in history can be taken at face value and as relevant also for the Christian church. In the light of the New Testament gospel, there is only one thing that can remain valid to the Christian faith in the Old Testament. That is the basic promise (*der Grundverheissung*): "I am the Lord, your God." Everything else is mere history of religion, possibly the object of archaeological fascination, but not evangelical theology. The reply of another Old Testament theologian, Claus Westermann, is hardly an overstatement: "Ultimately he [Baumgärtel] admits, then, that the church could also live without the Old Testament."[17] He hears in the Old Testament at best only an echo of what he has already and more clearly heard from the New Testament.

The group of scholars trained under von Rad at Heidelberg have ventured a positive reconciliation of the two versions of history, not by turning against their master, but by drawing out certain latent tendencies of his thought. Rolf Rendtorff is the Old Testament scholar in the Pannenberg group that is forging a new theology of historical revelation. We have already seen that in the field of New Testament studies they refused to make a choice between the historical Jesus and the kerygmatic Christ. The alternative itself had to be overcome by showing the mutually implicative character of kerygma and history. Likewise, in the Old Testament field they will not accept the view that we really have to choose between Israel's kerygmatic presentation of history and the modern critical-historical view of what happened. In the Old as in the New Testament, kerygma and history are bound up with each other. The historical facts are welded together with their inherent meanings in the narratives which Israel transmitted. Previous scholarship has operated with a sharp antithesis between fact and interpretation. Thus, it has been supposed that God revealed himself in the facts, and Israel placed upon these facts arbitrary interpretations of her own. Such a dichotomy between fact and interpretation cannot be maintained. Rendtorff points out that "the working out of the 'interpretation' is itself an historical event."[18] The history through which God revealed himself to Israel embraced the entire span of her historical experience. When, for example, Israel made her exodus out of Egypt, Israel's understanding of this event as divine redemption is as much a historical event as, say, the escape from the sea might have been.

Old Testament theology, according to Rendtorff, must include historical-critical research into the actual history of Israel. Israel's history itself has theological relevance, not only her kerygmatic witness to that history. At this point, Rendtorff goes beyond von Rad. The question is not whether we will accept the results of critical research or stand with Israel's confessional recital of her own history. To choose between the two would mean either the loss of the whole Old Testament or the loss of one's mind. Rendtorff's solution is better. "Rather we are confronted with the task of tracing the entire course from the first event to the final form of the tradition, in order that thereby we might make clear the historical significance of the event and of its history in Israel."[19] When we speak of the act of God in Israel's history, there is no reason to confine this activity to a few bare events that modern research can verify by cross-checking with other historical evidences. God's act is with the totality of Israel's career in history, including the highly complex and diverse ways in which she developed and transmitted her creedal traditions. The notion that we could strip away Israel's interpretation, begin from scratch with a naked historical reality, and reach a new understanding of that reality more fitting to the modern time has serious historical and theological objections against it.

The formula for reconciling the two versions of history that Rendtorff and Pannenberg have elevated to the rank of a category of interpretation significant for dogmatics is the concept of *Überlieferungsgeschichte*. The term is difficult to translate. Literally it means *tradition history*. Since, however, the word "tradition" in English often carries with it a static connotation, some have preferred the more fluid but awkward translation *transmission history*. What it means, basically, is the study of the dynamic historical process by which Israel transmitted her creedal testimonies to the acts of God. The concept has become especially important in Old Testament scholarship, but is obviously equally applicable to the traditions of the primitive Chris-

tian church. When scholars, building on the research of
Hermann Gunkel and Albrecht Alt, applied the methods
of form-critical analysis to the Old Testament, they discovered that all the historical traditions of Israel were impregnated with a confessional, kerygmatic interest. These
traditions proclaimed the acts of God in history. They
combined kerygmatic and liturgical impulses with historical factors. Then it became evident to scholars that
these traditions which were evolved over a long period of
time contained a variety of heterogeneous theological viewpoints.

How can there then be *a* theology of the Old Testament
when the various blocs of material build upon different
starting points, such as the patriarchal covenant, the exodus event, the Sinaitic or the Davidic covenant? Is there
no unity, no continuing connection between the various
reflections on the momentous episodes in Israel's history?
Did God act only from time to time, now and then, leaving
Israel to her own devices in the meantime? No. On closer
examination, patterns of meaning are discernible in the
various layers of tradition. A rhythm between promises and
fulfillments can be traced in the course of Israel's experience and understanding of her history. A single historical
episode could become the bearer of a number of different
theological interpretations because as Israel encountered
new situations, she actualized the meaning of that original
event in a new way. This is not necessarily a commentary
on the arbitrariness of her interpretations, but rather on
the inexhaustible meaning of the redemptive event which
God had performed. Thus, the various theologies are
united in the course of Israel herself, moving in the stream
of history from the past to the future, always actualizing
anew the meaning of what God had done in her past. The

whole history of Israel possesses a continuity through the discontinuity of times and sundry situations; the whole history, including the history of transmitting the redemptive events and their significances, is the act of God.

God's act cannot be confined to either of the two versions of history, neither in the single historical events in their bare nakedness (an absurd notion) nor in the dimension of kerygmatic portrayal of history's meaning. The two versions of history are really two dimensions of historical reality, the outer dimension of observable factual occurrence and the inner dimension in which the inherent meaning of the occurrence breaks into the consciousness of Israel. This inner dimension, as Rendtorff insists, is itself a historical event and also has a history. His summary statement is as follows: "In speaking of God's activity in the history of Israel we cannot be satisfied with the alternative between the two versions of history, the one produced by historical-critical research and the other portrayed by the Old Testament. For Israel's history occurred both in the outer events which are customarily the object of the critical study of history *and* in the various, stratified inner events which we bring together in the concept of tradition."[20]

TYPES OF OLD TESTAMENT INTERPRETATION

Most of the recent attempts to write a theology based on Old Testament traditions stress the point that the goal of Israel's history lies beyond itself in some future fulfillment. Israel's history cannot be fully understood out of itself, since in its own terms its ultimate meaning is anchored in an event to be consummated in the future. The faith of the New Testament is that Jesus Christ and his church are the authentic goal of the movement of history in the Old

Testament. Von Rad states with confidence as an Old Testament scholar that "we see everywhere in this history brought to pass by God's Word, in acts of judgment and acts of redemption alike, the prefiguration of the Christ event of the New Testament."[21]

It is a sign of health in Old Testament studies today that scholars do not write a "history of Israel" without going on to the theological question of its meaning for the Christian faith. From his side, the Old Testament theologian is showing how the New Testament presupposes the Old and is deeply grounded in it. In the heyday of late nineteenth-century liberalism, the Old Testament was studied exclusively from the point of view of the history of religions school. The Old Testament was the documentary source of the religion of Israel. It was possible to compare this religion to the Christian religion, for which the New Testament was the primary source document. One could trace the influence of the Jewish religion upon Christianity; or Christianity could be seen as the highest stage in a progressive development of religion. The basic connection between the Old and New Testaments had no permanent theological significance for the faith of the Christian church; it could be explained completely as a historical phenomenon within an evolutionary scheme.

The revolution in the history of modern theology symbolized by the name of Karl Barth spread into all fields of theology. The Old Testament was no exception, and I think it fair to say that the repercussions of this movement are still in force. The sign of this is that scholars in the field of Old Testament do not consider themselves "mere historians," but quite without apology think of themselves as theologians whose discipline forms an integral part of the totality of Christian theology. It is quite another question how they link the Old Testament to the Christian faith. The theological problem of the relation of the Old Testament to the New is a central concern of those involved in the current hermeneutical debate. With the staggering quantity of scholarly results before us from archaeological digging, literary analysis, form criticism, historical research, and traditio-historical study, the next step is to take inventory of all this from the perspective of what is specifically valid and relevant to the existential concerns of faith, of preaching, and of church instruction. That is what the hermeneutical discussion is all about. Here we can single out only a few lines along which this discussion is moving.

1. *The Christological interpretation of the Old Testament.* Karl Barth and Wilhelm Vischer have most emphatically carried through an interpretation of the Old Testament as witness to Jesus Christ. The revelation in the Old Testament is valid for us because in it Jesus Christ is manifest as the expected One.[22] Only the church can read the Old Testament rightly, but she reads it as the New Testament read it, as the witness to the coming of Christ. In the Old Testament, Jesus Christ is the object of expectation, in the New the object of recollection. "Since Old Testament and New Testament mutually witness to each other, they jointly witness to the one Jesus Christ."[23]

Wilhelm Vischer as an Old Testament scholar applied the dogmatic theses of Karl Barth at length in his three volumes entitled *The Witness of the Old Testament to Christ.*[24] This work has been hotly attacked and defended by scholars in many fields. The merit of this project, however, is that it dared to treat the Old Testament as a full partner with the New in the Christian canon. That poses a task for exegesis. If Jesus is really the Messiah, and if we believe that, then it is incumbent on us to show how Jesus fulfills the role of the Messiah promised and expected in the Old Testament. For the New Testament declares Jesus to be the Christ of the Old Testament. Vischer defines it this way: "The two main words of the Christian confession 'Jesus is the Christ'—the personal name 'Jesus' and the vocational name 'Christ'—correspond to the two parts of the Holy Scriptures: the New and the Old Testament. The Old Testament tells us *what* the Christ is; the New, *who* He is."[25]

Vischer's approach seemed all the more bold in view of his demand that a Christological exegesis must be controlled by modern philological and historical findings. At least in principle, Vischer expressed himself in favor of holding together both Karl Barth's theology of the Word of God and the new historical knowledge of Israel's traditions presented by scholars like Albrecht Alt and Johannes Pedersen. However, even many scholars who are in sympathy with Vischer's basic concern cannot but disclaim the somewhat exaggerated ways in which he has carried through his Christologizing of the Old Testament. Barth himself has expressed reservations about the details, but urges those who criticize Vischer to try to perform the same task better.[26]

A favorite ploy in discrediting a Christological approach to the Old Testament is to point to its extreme results in Vischer's work. However, it is possible to retain Vischer's thesis as genuinely expressive of an article of faith, even while rejecting the extreme applications to which it might lead. Jesus Christ is the goal of the Old Testament, and in some sense also its content. This does not mean that the exegete must ask of every Old Testament text: What does it say about Christ? Luther's hermeneutical principle which calls for the texts to be interpreted as "bearers of Christ"[27] can be misleading if one supposes that every text is valid only to the extent that somehow or other one can find Christological content in it. Such a wooden application of a Christological criterion can only drive the exegete into an allegorical type of exegesis which finds depths of meaning in the texts that the original authors never imagined were there. Then the historical distance and material difference between the Old and New Testaments are played down, and once again the specifically Old Testament word is blocked from coming to expression in the church today.

The rightful concern to hold to the unity of the two Testaments must be carefully distinguished from tendencies to merge or identify them. The Christological approach is appropriate within limits, but it cannot be the only one. It is in danger of accomplishing too much and too little; too much because it tends to read in Messianic content where it does not exist, and too little, for the Old Testament traditions cannot be profitably reduced solely to their witness to Christ. On historical grounds this is easy to establish. But even on dogmatic grounds it is suspect if it claims a monopoly on the hermeneutical avenues into the Old Testament. The God who is operative in the Old Testament is the Father of Jesus Christ. And the Old Testament as well as the New bears witness to God as Spirit. It is a legitimate question of dogmatics, which we cannot pursue here, whether, and to what extent, the Christian doctrine of the Trinity has its roots also in the Old Testament. This doctrine may serve to warn us against a modern tendency to reduce the total Biblical witness to the second article of the Creed.

2. *The existentialist interpretation of the Old Testament.* Rudolf Bultmann and, to some extent, Friedrich Baumgärtel have made the strongest case for interpreting

the Old Testament as witness to human existence under the law. The Lutheran category of law and gospel is here linked to an existentialist view of man and salvation. We shall see what this means for the Old Testament and its unity with the New.

First, Bultmann rejects the traditional view of the Old Testament as a book of prophecies that are fulfilled in the New Testament. This has been made impossible by our modern methods of historical science. Besides, when the New Testament discovered prophecies in the Old Testament, we can now show that this was done by reading them into the Old Testament as a result of fulfillment. The motive for doing this was polemical in relation to the Jews and apologetic in relation to the Gentiles.[28] Arguments for the truth of the salvation event in Christ were strengthened by appealing to the antiquity of the Messianic prophecies in the Old Testament. Bultmann feels that such arguments are only attempts to gain security for faith and thus subtract from the real stumbling block, the offense of the cross of Jesus, which faith has to overcome in its own way, apart from objective proofs. Faith, as Bultmann conceives it, has no use for historical evidences that Jesus Christ is the goal of the prophetic history of Israel.

By a study of the concepts of covenant, the Kingdom of God, and the people of God in the Old Testament, Bultmann comes to the conclusion that each contains an internal contradiction which prevents its realization within history. Israel, for example, conceived of herself as a covenant people under God's rule as a real, empirical, historical entity in this world. However, in the New Testament these concepts are radically eschatologized. Thus Bultmann can say that in the New Testament the "community is not a people as a historical entity within the world. . . . The new covenant is a radically eschatological dimension, that is, a dimension outside the world, and to belong to it takes its members out of the world. . . . The rule of God and so of Christ . . . is eschatological and supramundane in its entirety; and the man who has a part in it is, as it were, already taken out of the world. . . . The people of God is no longer an empirical historical entity—it does not exist as a people requiring institutional ordinance for its organization."[29] In his book *History and Eschatology,* Bultmann again insists on the eschatological difference between the Old and New Testament conceptions. "*The New Covenant* is not grounded on an event of the history of the people as was the Old Covenant. . . . *The new people of God* has no real history, for it is the community of the end-time, an eschatological phenomenon."[30] We have cited these passages from Bultmann to show why Bultmann breaks all revelational continuity between the history of God's people in the Old Testament and the new people of God in the New. The reason lies in his concept of eschatology.

Is it really true that in the New Testament the concept of eschatology can be set in simple antithesis to history? Hardly! In the New Testament, too, the church lives horizontally in time; it knows of the differences between past, present, and future; it exists as the new community in this world with all its very concrete problems and pains; its life in Christ does not disrupt all continuity with the continuous history of God with his people in the Old Testament; its sacred Scriptures are the Old Testament; what God has done in Jesus Christ is decisive also for the destiny of the Jews. Romans, chs. 9 to 11, stands against Bultmann's sharp distinction between Old Testament history and New Testament eschatology.

Bultmann does, however, find meaning in the Old Testament, not in spite of but because of the contradictions he cites. The meaning of the Old Testament is negative.

Bultmann calls Old Testament history a "miscarriage of history."[31] This history of miscarriage may be considered as "law" because the law reveals man's contradictions and drives him to Christ. In this sense the Old Testament may be considered a preparation for the gospel, as a revelation of Israel's failure.

Bultmann claims the authority of Paul and Luther for his bracketing the whole Old Testament as law. And no doubt he is partly right. The question, however, is whether the law/gospel dialectic is the exclusively valid hermeneutic of the Old Testament. It cannot be convincingly argued that Paul and Luther narrowed their entire treatment of the Old Testament down to this perspective. To be sure, the demand of God becomes concrete in the Old Testament and the grace of God becomes overwhelming in the New Testament, but there is more than law in the Old and grace in the New. If there were only law in the Old Testament, then Bultmann would be right in saying, "Hence, it can be only for *pedagogical reasons* that the Christian Church uses the Old Testament to make man conscious of standing under God's demand."[32] Only for pedagogical reasons! And obviously, for the law which the gospel presupposes "by no means needs to be the concrete Old Testament."[33] The demands of the law are universally present and operative in human existence. As Bultmann says, "They are grounded in human relationship itself."[34] We may use the Old Testament today as a mirror of our existence under the law. There are many valid and unforgettable illustrations of sin and the need for grace in the Old Testament. No doubt this is true, but is that all that the church finds in the Old Testament?

Bultmann himself is aware that the New Testament and the Christian church have held to the Old Testament as God's word of revelation. And Bultmann also knows that in the Old Testament itself the grace of God is a constant theme. "The Law, as such, is a demonstration of the grace of God."[35] Ideas of sin and grace, repentance and forgiveness are very similar in both Testaments. Yet, despite all similarities, the contrast between the Old and the New is so great that Bultmann cannot allow that the Old Testament is God's Word of revelation to Christian faith. "For the person who stands within the Church the history of Israel is a closed chapter. The Christian proclamation cannot and may not remind hearers that God led their fathers out of Egypt, that he once led the people into captivity and brought them back again into the land of the Promise, that he restored Jerusalem and the Temple, and so on. Israel's history is not our history, and in so far as God has shown his grace in that history, such grace is not meant for us. . . . This means, however, that *to us the history of Israel is not history of revelation.* The events which meant something for Israel, which were God's Word, mean nothing more to us."[36] In another summary statement, Bultmann states in comparable bluntness: "To the Christian faith the Old Testament is not in the true sense God's Word. So far as the Church proclaims the Old Testament as God's Word, it just finds in it again what is already known from the revelation in Jesus Christ."[37]

It would be difficult to imagine that Luther's formula of law and gospel was ever so intended as a hermeneutical device to negate the value of the Old Testament as God's Word of revelation to the church and mankind in all places and for all time. The unfortunate thing is that while the law/gospel formula is a helpful way of bringing out the difference between the Old and New Testaments, Bultmann's application of it has undermined the very historical foundations on which the formula must stand to make sense. And thus the overarching unity of the Bible as the medium of divine revelation is broken. As so often, Bultmann's brilliant insights, most of which can be gratefully accepted, are smothered by an avalanche of surprising and, to us, unfounded conclusions which quite understandably have evoked dissent, and in some quarters, even the category of heresy against him.

3. *The typological interpretation of the Old Testament.* Gerhard von Rad, Hans Walter Wolff, and others establish continuity between the Old and New Testaments by the use of the typological method. In his programmatic essay, *Typological Interpretation of the Old Testament,* von Rad defines its aim, limits, and possibilities. The typological way of thinking seeks to discover a relation of correspondence between certain types in the Old Testament, such as persons, institutions, or events, which foreshadow similar realities, or antitypes, in the New Testament.

The new typologists are anxious to distinguish typology from allegory. The difference lies in the greater historical sense of the typological way of thinking. Walther Eichrodt points out why the two methods should not be lumped together. "For typology, the historical value of the text to be interpreted forms the essential presupposition for the use of it. For allegory, on the contrary, this is indifferent or even offensive, and must be pushed to one side to make room for the 'spiritual' sense which lies behind."[38]

Mindful that a renewal of typology might draw the interpreter's attention to a host of insignificant details that can be made to correspond in the two Testaments, von Rad gives it a clear Christological focus. There is one basic analogy between the Old and New Testaments, namely, between God's redemptive work in the Old Covenant and the Christ event in the New. At this point the Christological and typological methods of interpretation coincide. Each has need of the other. The premise on which the typological method rests is that the same God who acted in Christ "left his footprints in the history of the Old Testament covenant people."[39] The correspondence between type and antitype has further hermeneutical consequences. First, the context for interpreting the Old Testament texts in their fullness must be the New Testament fulfillment. As strange as it may sound, Old Testament interpretation must go beyond the Old Testament. The theologian must purposely look for prerepresentations of the New Testament witness to Christ. Secondly, not only the similarities but also the differences between the type and antitype must be sought. The fulfillment outruns the expectation; the types turn out to be pale glimmerings compared to the splendor, the *doxa,* reflected by the antitypical occurrences. Typology can thus be an aid in defining the relation of the Old Testament to the New, portraying both their unity and their difference.

The typological exegesis of the Old Testament is not, however, by itself an adequate method of interconnecting the Old and New Testaments. It is not enough, as Wolfhart Pannenberg points out, to establish "structural agreements"[40] between the Christ event and the Old Testament. Pannenberg does not deny that certain analogies do exist. Their validity, however, rests upon the one history worked by God which includes both Testaments. Typological interpretation *of itself* would tend to become unhistorical, satisfied with superficial verbal or conceptual similarities between the Old Testament type and the New Testament counterpart. Therefore, all the new typologists to my knowledge ground their interpretation in the Biblical theology of history. Here the real unity of the Old Testament with the New is seen in the great flow of history which moves from promise to fulfillment. History itself as the work of the revealing God is the real basis for all the typological comparisons one finds in the two halves of the Bible.

4. *The historical interpretation of the Old Testament.* Walther Zimmerli, Wolfhart Pannenberg, and others who follow the lead of Gerhard von Rad have adopted the promise/fulfillment scheme of interlocking the two Testaments. This type of interpretation may be called "historical" if we are careful not to allow the secular view of positivistic historicism to determine what is meant by history. For this reason the concept of history employed in the promise/fulfillment scheme is often modified by words like "elective," "prophetic," "eschatological," "revelatory," "redemptive," "holy," "sacred," and so on. This is history qualified by the view of the divine plan for the world and mankind that we find in major sectors of the Bible. The German word *Heilsgeschichte* is perhaps used more often than any other in referring to the peculiarly Biblical understanding of history as the ongoing redemptive activity of God.

Von Rad, having this kind of history in mind, has called the Old Testament a "history book."[41] It is a history directed by the creative Word of God in which we can discern "a whole pattern of mutually corresponding prophetic promises and divine fulfillments."[42] Von Rad himself has seen the danger of a one-sided kerygmatic interpretation of the Old Testament, which asks for meanings irrespective of their rootedness in historical events. The Old Testament is a history not only of Israel's religious *faith,* but of God's *activity* in the real situations of Israel's earthly existence.

Walther Zimmerli has most carefully worked out the relationship between the Old and the New Testaments in the language of promise and fulfillment. The category promise/fulfillment is inseparably bound to a history extending forward and backward along a temporal continuum. Zimmerli is critical of the existentialist dissolution of history as temporal extension into the "historicity" of existence. The "yesterday" and the "tomorrow" of history are unhinged from the all-significant "now" of each passing moment. In contrast, the promise/fulfillment category "guards against every flight into a timeless, mystical understanding of God's nearness, as well as against an understanding of encounter with God reduced to a single existentialistic point without historical relatedness."[43] In an eloquent passage, Zimmerli writes: "When we survey the entire Old Testament, we find ourselves involved in a great history of movement from promise toward fulfillment. It flows like a large brook—here rushing swiftly, there apparently coming to rest in a quiet backwater, and yet moving forward as a whole toward a distant goal which lies beyond itself."[44]

The goal that lies in the Old Testament's future is Jesus Christ, the good news that the promises have been fulfilled. Yet, in the New Testament the believers in Christ are caught up in a new state of waiting. The final fulfillment has occurred unsurpassably and unrepeatably in Christ; yet the life of faith stretches forward in hope toward a more glorious unveiling of Christ. The end of history has happened; yet history runs on. Christians live "in a new way under an arc of tension between promise and fulfillment."[45] When Jesus Christ is called the end of the Old Testament, this does not mean that the Old Testament sinks into oblivion for Christians. He is the end of the Old Testament as its fulfillment. The word "end" is ambiguous, meaning either "goal" or "terminus." The eschatological significance of Christ does not put an end to the Old Testament; rather Christ is revealed as the end purpose of the stretch of history in the Old Testament.

Of all the hermeneutical approaches we have discussed so far, it would seem to us that the promise/fulfillment scheme has the surest grasp of the real basis for the necessity of the Old Testament for Christian faith and of its relation to the New. And yet without the others it would tend to become formalistic and abstract, verging on a religious philosophy of history. The Christological approach will make clear that the Old Testament and the New together converge upon Jesus Christ, the beginning and the end. In the words of von Rad, "Christ is given to us only through the double witness of the choir of those who await and those who remember."[46] The existentialist view of the Old Testament which enters into dialogue with it to discover what man is and how he is to exist can assuredly redound to the benefit of faith and preaching. Also the application of the Pauline-Lutheran dialectic of law and gospel to the Old Testament can sharpen the eyes of faith to the marvelously new thing God has brought to pass in Jesus Christ. But all of this degenerates into mere religious anthropology without the solid foundation of historical reality undergirding it. Finally, the typological method of exegesis can put flesh on the skeletal outline of a theology of history spanning the distances between promises and fulfillments in the Bible. Its advantage is that it can search in greater detail for significant correspondences and connections between Old and New Testament phenomena. The four hermeneutical avenues into the Old Testament may mutually support each other and enrich our understanding of the one history of salvation that begins to unfold in the Old Testament and reaches its zenith in the resurrection of Jesus Christ.

Chapter VI

Hermeneutics of the Word and Church

From Schleiermacher to Bultmann

There are two great gaps to be bridged in the salvation of mankind. We might call the first the vertical gap between God and man. This first gap is in turn qualified by a twofold separation described by the Christian doctrines of the creation and the fall of man. When God created man as a creature of time, man was separated from the eternity of God. The story of the fall of man points to a second and more radical separation, namely, between the holiness of God and the sinfulness of man. Christians believe that this vertical gap—in both dimensions—has been closed definitively by God in Jesus Christ. The incarnation of the Son of God represents the inbreaking of eternity into time; the atonement is the work of the Holy God reconciling a rebellious world unto himself. In theological language, we commonly call this total activity of God in bridging the vertical chasm "the Christ event." This Christ event should be the ultimate concern of every person.

However, the Christ event happened at a particular time and place, two thousand years ago in Palestine. Here we face what we might call the horizontal gap, the second great gap. How should the Christ event be transmitted to us today in its wholeness of reality and meaning? There is a temporal gap between the past and the present, and not only that, but the culture, world view, and way of thinking of first-century Christians are quite different from our own. Hermeneutics, a vogue word today, is the science of reflecting on how a word or event in a past time and culture may be understood and become existentially meaningful in our present situation. Heremeneutical reflection enters into the problem of the horizontal gap.

In modern theology a lively debate is taking place on hermeneutics. Gerhard Ebeling and Ernst Fuchs have used the term so frequently and with such an elasticity of meaning that their position is commonly referred to as "the new hermeneutic" or simply "the hermeneutical school."[1] Actually, however, the hermeneutical discussion cuts across party lines and involves those who stand at opposite poles of theology. It is also evident that the terms of the present debate are not only defined by Bultmann's use of Heidegger's hermeneutical categories, but also have roots in a prior development beginning with Schleiermacher and running through Dilthey.

Traditionally, hermeneutics dealt with the rules to be observed in Biblical exegesis. Today it enjoys a wider reference. Hermeneutics is a fundamental inquiry into the conditions which must obtain in the understanding of history or historical documents. Thus, it embraces both the methodological rules to be applied in exegesis as well as the epistemological presuppositions of historical understanding. When the accent falls on the latter meaning, hermeneutics could be called a "critique of historical reason" in the sense in which Dilthey used this expression,[2] namely, as investigation of the possibility of understanding documents that reach us from the past. The enlargement of the scope of hermeneutics from regulative principles of analysis to the art of interpreting historical documents to disclose their meaning for us today is often traced back to Schleiermacher.

Friedrich Schleiermacher realized that more is required to *understand* the Biblical texts than the mere application of the methods of literary and historical analysis. The objective analysis must be joined with an intuitive grasp of a work as the life expression of its author. Schleiermacher rightly saw that the hermeneutical problem of bridging the horizontal gap between what the text has to say and our life today cannot be solved by the critical-historical method alone. But his solution to supplement the grammatical-historical approach by a psychological interpretation, that is, by an imaginative reproduction of the creative art by which the work was originally produced, bars him from an appropriate interpretation of the text for two reasons: (1) the historical gap between the author's past and our present cannot be bridged by a psychological act, for although the author and the interpreter do have a susceptibility for common experiences, by virtue of their common human nature, the method of psychological re-creation cannot take account of the differences between historical situations; (2) what the Biblical text intends to express is not, after all, the inner feeling of the author's soul; rather, what the author has to say is supposed to be valid quite apart from the psychic conditions which accompany his utterances. Thus, psychological interpretation, from the standpoint of the author's own intention, is quite beside the point; it shifts the object of understanding from the content of the text to the process by which the text sprang out of the author's inwardness.

Wilhelm Dilthey further developed Schleiermacher's psychological hermeneutics. He agreed that the interpreter must reexperience the original creative moment in which an author gave expression to life. He grasped more clearly, however, that historical events in the past must be read as expressions of historical life. With this suggestion the scope of hermeneutics was potentially broadened to take account of the significance of historical events. The historian today is able to interpret the past because all historical events are effects of the human spirit in whose structures and capacities the historian also participates. The person who *writes* history is the same kind of being as the one who *makes* history—otherwise historical knowledge would be an impossibility.[3]

By and large, however, Dilthey's hermeneutical conception did not escape the limitations of Schleiermacher's psychological mold. The dimension of the Scriptural witness to God's activity in history could not be encompassed by this approach. No doubt this accounts in part for the negative attitude Schleiermacher held toward the Old Testament. The Old Testament as a "book of history" is not congenial to a psychological interpretation of religion. The psychological approach of Schleiermacher and Dilthey reduces the understanding of a historical document to possibilities of experience which the author and the interpreter have in common. But what about the uncommon and the difference? That would seem to be ruled out a priori. The Scriptures then are heard only as an echo of universally human possibilities of experience. That which is new and unrepeatable in history as the medium of divine activity can scarcely be accommodated by a psychologically determined hermeneutics.

Rudolf Bultmann's grasp of the hermeneutical problem retains continuity with Schleiermacher and Dilthey.[4] He finds that they have properly focused on the presupposition of all historical interpretation, namely, the basic experiential consanguinity of the author and the interpreter of a text. Bultmann sees the importance of defining that presupposition more clearly. He too approaches the Biblical text with a given view of the structure of human existence and its possibilities. An element of this structure is man's involvement in history as one who questions and who is addressed. The presupposition at work in historical interpretation is "the interpreter's relationship in his life to the subject which is directly or indirectly expressed in the text."[5] A document will read differently whether one goes at it with a political, aesthetic, or religious interest. This interest shapes the question which one brings to the text and to which the text will respond. Bultmann has rightly reacted against naïve historicism which pretends that historical research can be carried on without any presuppositions. Every historian's interpretation of the past is guided by a preunderstanding. This makes it all the more urgent to be self-critical about the role of the preunderstanding that is appropriate in Biblical interpretation. Not every preapprehension is equally fitting in Biblical interpretation. The question is whether Bultmann's concept of existential self-understanding is not too limiting as a hermeneutical principle.

Bultmann states: "The interpretation of biblical writings is not subject to conditions different from those applying to all other kinds of literature."[6] This assertion of far-reaching consequence has worked like a sovereign axiom in modern hermeneutics. The older distinction between sacred and profane hermeneutics broke down with the rise of the critical-historical method and the demise of Protestant Orthodoxy's dogmatic control of exegesis. Since then theologians have been claiming a kind of scientific neutrality for their methods of interpretation. This, however, has brought about an internal weakening of the specifically Biblical content that does not fit into our preconceived molds. Something like a revival of the older distinction between profane and sacred elements in Biblical hermeneutics is essential. It would seem more honest for theologians to acknowledge that in Biblical interpretation they *do* bring a preunderstanding which is conditioned by experiences and interests that are far from universally human. Besides general philosophical and historical aspects of hermeneutics, there is a theological dimension that presupposes the hearing of the Word, believing in the church (*credo . . . sanctam ecclesiam catholicam*), and the personal insight of faith. We have entitled this chapter "Hermeneutics of the Word and Church" to indicate that in Biblical interpretation a preunderstanding is active that has been powerfully shaped by the living Word in the tradition of the church.

It would seem to us that the Achilles' heel of Bultmann's hermeneutical proposal is his narrow conception of the preunderstanding appropriate in Biblical interpretation. Is this preunderstanding given with human existence as such, or is it not qualified by the understanding of faith given in the community of believers? Bultmann thinks the former is the case. The Heidelberg philosopher, Hans-Georg Gadamer, correctly observes, however, that although Bultmann claims general validity for his preunderstanding on the grounds of existentialist philosophy, he nevertheless actually operates with a preunderstanding impregnated by theological assumptions.[7] When these theological assumptions are brought out into the open and confronted by the Biblical material, they prove to be too confining.

Because Bultmann does not include all the specifically theological links in the hermeneutical chain that connect the text and the interpreter, the content of the text is reduced to an existentialist interpretation which looks only for the understanding of existence reflected in the text. The magnitude of the text's message is restricted by the a priori decision that what is relevant in the text is only that which can be understood beforehand as a possibility of human existence. Under such a restriction it is doubtful that the text will be allowed to say all that it intends to say. At least to many ordinary readers and countless theologians the New Testament, not to mention the Old Testament, is concerned about many other things besides possibilities of human existence, such as the will of God in history and his works in the world. The New Testament statements about God, the world, history, society, and the church cannot be understood as mere corollaries of faith's understanding of human existence and its possibilities. The reverse is the Biblical order of thought. The right understanding of existence and its possibilities is dependent on the knowledge of God, of his revelation through history, and his plan for the church and the world.

The upshot of what we have said is that hermeneutics which traces out the conditions for a full hearing of the Scriptural word cannot rest *exclusively* on the allegedly neutral pillars of an existentialist philosophical system and the critical-historical method. Theology in the form of dogmatics will *also* perform an essential service by showing how the preunderstanding implicated in Biblical interpretation is concretely determined by what the history of the Bible as the canon has meant in the tradition of the church and in the lives of believers, and in what sense the Bible is to be read as the unique medium of the message of God's salvatory action. Dogmatics will also perform a critical function in hermeneutics by detecting prejudices at work behind the scene in Biblical interpretation which force the text to adjust to an all too narrowly preconceived framework. Hermeneutics will work to enable the subject matter of the text in its pastness and otherness to come to expression, even though it might spring the prior framework of the interpreter's preunderstanding. In the history of Protestant theology, dogmatics has received the bad reputation of lording it over the Bible, prejudging what it has to say; historical and philosophical criticism in undermining dogmatics received the glorious reputation as liberators of the Bible. Now it seems that the roles might well be reversed. Dogmatics will have to assert itself both constructively and critically, taking its place in the arena of the debate on hermeneutics as a full partner with other disciplines, to broaden the terms of the discussion and clear the way for understanding the message of the Bible in its fullness.

NEWER HERMENEUTICAL OPTIONS

Bultmann's pioneer probing of the hermeneutical question has been followed up in different ways by Ernst Fuchs, Gerhard Ebeling, Heinrich Ott, and Wolfhart Pannenberg. They are presenting us with a variety of newer hermeneutical options. Fuchs and Ebeling, working together as a team, seek to go beyond Bultmann; Ott attempts to mediate between his two mentors, Barth and Bultmann; and Pannenberg proposes to place hermeneutics on a quite new track.

Fuchs and Ebeling have followed Bultmann in making the theme of hermeneutics an indispensable auxiliary in a theology of the Word of God. Hermeneutics is defined as the theory of understanding the movement of the Word of God from the Biblical text to the proclamation in the present time. Preaching today is the goal of exegesis and hermeneutical reflection. The oral character of the Word is decisive. The Word is an "acoustical event." This aspect of the Word became frozen in Protestant orthodoxy as its doctrine of verbal inspiration equated the Word with the words of the Bible. For Ebeling and Fuchs, hermeneutics as a theory of understanding must really be a theory about language, for understanding is not merely reflection *about* words, but happens as an event through words.[8] Hermeneutics is to make understanding through language an event. Therefore, it is indispensable to theology and preaching, for the gospel is a word event.

In Ebeling's thought, hermeneutics is no longer conceived of as a neutral or profane method of reflection; it has become theological. Actually, as James Robinson has pointed out, the hermeneutical thinking of Ebeling and Fuchs is "coterminous with Christian theology as the statement of the meaning of Scripture for our day."[9] He claims further that "the new hermeneutic is a new theology, just as were dialectical theology and Ritschlianism before it."[10] Hence, theological hermeneutics is a doctrine of the Word of God becoming event again and again within the sphere of human language; it reflects on the process by which the text becomes sermon, that is, a new linguistic occurrence of the Word of God.

Ebeling and Fuchs are critical of the main line in Bultmann's hermeneutics which asks us to go beneath the language of a text to the understanding of existence which it enshrines. This shift of interest from existential understanding to linguistic event parallels the turn in Martin Heidegger's philosophy from existentialism to ontology, that is, from an existentialist analysis of *Dasein* which sees language as a secondary objectification of the understanding given with existence to an understanding of man whose language is the primal, nonobjectifying voice of being. Heidegger calls language "the house of being." The rediscovery of the hermeneutical import of language is an important advance beyond Bultmann. It places a high premium on the word of proclamation as a hermeneutical vehicle of the Word of God.

As Bultmann interrogates the New Testament texts for expressions of inauthentic and authentic existence, Fuchs finds in them utterances of inauthentic or authentic language. Man is by nature a linguistic being, answering the call of being. This call comes to man through history, for history is basically the history of language, of being coming to expression through language. The coming of the Word of God is understood as the coming of true language, the language of love, especially in Jesus' language of love. As such, Jesus can be called the "language event." At this point we find the primary theological motive for Ebeling's and Fuchs's renewal of the quest for the historical Jesus. They must get back to the authentic language of Jesus himself—the language of faith.

If the movement of linguistic hermeneutics on the one side is back to the historical Jesus, on the other side its movement is forward into the "world come of age" which requires a new language, a "non-religious interpretation of Biblical concepts."[11] The hermeneutical problem includes the unfinished task of translation not in the superficial sense of reduplicating the words of one language into more or less equivalent words of another language, but in the sense of a radical transference of meaning, a transculturation of the Word into new words. Ebeling and Fuchs agree with Heidegger that we are living in a time of counterfeit language, of inauthentic speech, when the language of the Western tradition has degenerated into the corruptible, objectifying language of a technological society that turns man into an object to be controlled and manipulated like other things.

We must question whether language should be singled out as the exclusively valid vehicle of the Biblical revelation. What happens to history as a result? There is cause for some complaint when Jesus is called a "language event" and the significance of his person is equated with the power of his language to affect other persons. Such an approach to Jesus of Nazareth will be especially favorably inclined to the texts that transmit the parables of Jesus. But it will scarcely do justice to the historic events that play a decisive role in the course of Jesus' life, particularly the denouement in the crucifixion and resurrection. Good Friday and Easter Sunday were not merely "language events." They were historic events creative of language, and revelatory of God only when the historic action and its linguistic vehicle are kept indissolubly together, with neither side being collapsed into the other. Neither will the concept of language grasp more than a part of the hermeneutical action of bridging the chasm of the centuries that lie between the Christ event and contemporary life. The hermeneutical power of the Sacraments as vehicles of the self-contemporization of Jesus Christ is not fully explicable as a linguistic phenomenon.

Heinrich Ott has also made the concern of hermeneutics intensely his own. As Karl Barth's disciple and successor, he has inherited an imposing dogmatic of the Word of God. The problem for Ott is one of *understanding* the Word of God. To this end he proposes that we must go farther in the direction of the human, as Barth himself has done in one of his later works, *The Humanity of God*.

Dogmatics must become hermeneutically oriented if its concern is not only for the truth of God's Word but also for its understandability, including its preachability, in the human realm. Ott's attention to this problem of understanding the Word of God has made him lean toward Bultmann and Heidegger, to the dismay of his fellow Barthians. Ott tries to find points of reconciliation between Barth and Bultmann. To Bultmann belongs the credit for having made the hermeneutical question inescapable for us and for demonstrating the unavoidability of ontological questions in theology. Barth, on the other hand, has given undivided attention to the explication of the Word of God as dogmatics' standard for testing the preaching of the church today. Ott believes it possible to combine the basic concerns of Bultmann and Barth.

Ott has sketched out the main lines of his dogmatic program in his book *Theology and Preaching*,[12] written in the form of a commentary on the Heidelberg Catechism. Here he makes it clear that dogmatics performs an essential function in hermeneutical reflection. The chief assignment of dogmatics is to facilitate the movement from the Bible to preaching. Preaching the gospel is the constitutive function of the church, and dogmatics is "the reflexive function of preaching itself."[13] Dogmatics exists only because the church exists, and the church exists to preach the gospel. Preaching and dogmatics exist in continuity with each other. Both presuppose the faith of the church and both have the gospel of Christ as their common subject matter. Ott says, "Dogmatics is preaching to the preachers."[14] The unity of dogmatics and preaching lies in the one, indivisible kerygma from which they both derive. Their difference lies in their respective modes of expression. Dogmatics inquires into the unity, the totality, and the intelligibility of the Biblical kerygma, elaborating this in a comprehensive, systematic way. Preaching, on the other hand, always deals with the Biblical text *ad hoc*, relating the whole kerygma "one-sidedly" to a concrete situation.

In sharing Bultmann's hermeneutical concern, Ott is continually asking how genuine preaching is possible today. By genuine preaching he means proclamation that enables an act of understanding spanning the gulf between the Biblical message and human existence today. He uses the figure of the "hermeneutical arch" to describe the continuum of understanding that stretches back to what the Biblical texts have to say and forward to the sermon in the present situation. "A single arch stretches from the Biblical texts to the contemporary preaching of the church."[15] Dogmatics stands in the middle of the arch between exegesis and homiletics, that is, between the text and the sermon. "Dogmatics . . . lifted out of the 'hermeneutical arch,' isolated on the one side from exegesis and on the other from preaching, immediately becomes an understanding without foundation."[16] Philosophy also forms a part of the hermeneutical arch. The philosophy of existence helps the preacher and theologian to understand the concrete existence of men today. Genuine preaching must give an answer to a genuine, existential question of man. It would seem to us that, at this point, Ott has stretched his Barthian loyalty to the breaking point. He has veered closer to Emil Brunner's idea of the point of contact (*Anknüpfungspunkt*) between God and man, to Tillich's method of correlating kerygma and situation, and Bultmann's concept of the existential preunderstanding. Yet he admits the danger of allowing specific philosophical presuppositions to determine the scope and content of the theological explication of the gospel.

The bedrock of the dialectic of question and answer which Ott now proposes as a hermeneutical principle, and which Brunner, Tillich, and Bultmann express in their different ways, is the law/gospel principle in classic Lutheran theology. Ebeling, in particular, vigorously asserts that the pattern of all theological thought may be construed in terms of "law and gospel."[17] Ott, on the other hand, seeks to deny the validity of this principle for his own thinking. "I myself am in a position to enter upon another path, since I—as a Reformed theologian and a pupil of Karl Barth—do not think on the premise of the law-gospel pattern."[18] I would suggest, however, that Ott either does not realize or does not admit the extent to which his own thinking has departed from the Barthian pattern of thinking. His fellow Barthians who accuse him of betraying the consistency of the Barthian method, which holds to a reversal of the law/gospel dialectic, rightly see that his move in the direction of Heidegger, his acceptance of the hermeneutical question as formulated by Bultmann, and his appeal for an existentialist interpretation of the kerygma are all symptomatic of a break with the Barthian way of thinking.[19] Ott actually thinks in the pattern of the law/gospel dialectic, even though as a pupil of Barth he wishes to deny it.

Ott's willingness to accept the idea of a positive relation between philosophy and theology implicates him in the law/gospel dialectic of Lutheran theology. This seems transparently clear in his little book *Verkündigung und Existenz,* in which he correlates existentialist philosophy to theology in terms of the question/answer dialectic. When he says that preaching must answer to a real existential concern of man, he is saying in effect that the gospel addresses man who is under the law. Man under the law can be the object of existentialist analysis. Theology and preaching need the help of the philosophy of existence in order to open their eyes to the real questions of the man to whom the gospel is addressed. This is clearly an instance of thinking in the pattern of the law/gospel dialectic. This makes room for the notion that philosophy also has a job to do toward a theological hermeneutic. As a pretheological discipline, philosophy's role will remain limited and marginal. If philosophy is allowed the upper hand, theology is secularized; if, however, philosophy is eliminated, theology is introverted. The law/gospel dialectic calls for a working relation between philosophy and theology for the sake of a hermeneutic that must learn from two books, the book of Holy Scripture and the book of human experience in the world.

Wolfhart Pannenberg seeks to answer the hermeneutical problem in terms of a theology of world history.[20] We have shown in previous chapters how, for Pannenberg, the category of history is decisive in the solution of theological problems, whether we are dealing with the idea of revelation, the resurrection of Jesus, or the significance of the Old Testament. So also, history is the key to his hermeneutical theory. The hermeneutical problem is constituted by the fact that a wide gulf exists between the Biblical world of thought and that of our own time. The modern historical method of exegesis requires us to interpret a text in the sense in which it was originally meant. The more sharply we put the historical question of meaning to the text, the more conscious we become of our distance from the intellectual world of the text. Hermeneutics should assist theology and preaching to express the full Biblical content in the contemporary context. A mere repristination of the words and ideas of the Bible or of the Reformation will not close the gap between the Biblical witnesses and our own time.

In answer to the question, "How can the distance between the past of the texts and the present of the interpreter be bridged?"[21] Pannenberg picks up an image offered by Hans-Georg Gadamer, the image of "merging horizons." The horizon of the present-day interpreter must be enlarged sufficiently to encompass the horizon of the text to be interpreted. The historical difference between the horizon of a particular past age and the horizon of our own contemporary outlook must not be overlooked, but rather overbridged. Liberalism tends to commit the error of dissolving the particularity of the past into the dominant ethos of the present time; fundamentalism commits the reverse error of submerging the distinctive problems of the present into the world view of a primitive age. The hermeneutical task is that of finding an overarching perspective that can bring the horizons of the past and present together without obliterating their distinctive characteristics. Bultmann's demythologizing program and Bonhoeffer's appeal for a nonreligious interpretation of the gospel are two responses to this hermeneutical task. Pannenberg doubts that either one solves the problem. Something is lost in the translation; theology ceases to be theology. In Bultmann's case, theology has all but passed over into anthropology, and those who have responded most enthusiastically to Bonhoeffer's challenge have inclined toward a liberal humanism.

If the hermeneutical gap between primitive Christianity and our own age can be closed neither by a secularization of the gospel (liberalism) nor by a repristination of Biblical ideas (fundamentalism), what other alternative is there? Pannenberg's answer is in terms of a theology of universal

history (*Universalgeschichte*). "Thus the present situation
may be related to that of early Christianity in terms of that
horizon which alone connects both without blurring their
differences, namely, the horizon of the *historical process*.
The hermeneutical difference between the traditional texts
and our present time would be at once respected and super-
seded in a concept of the *history* connecting both, if this
history can again be regarded as the work of the Biblical
God."[22] The concept of history as tradition-history (*Überlieferungsgeschichte*) which the Pannenberg school has developed as the unifying bridge of Old and New Testament
traditions is now transposed to church history and world
history. The totality of history—Old and New Testament
history, church and world history—is incorporated into a
Christian theology of history. The universal-historical conception of reality as a unity is rooted and grounded in the
Biblical concept of *one* God. Theology that bases itself on
the Biblical revelation of God has no right to partition
off a segment of reality as its private concern, and dismiss
the rest of reality to the fragmentary interests of secular
disciplines. Pannenberg calls theology a universal science
because there is no aspect of reality or knowledge of truth
which can be ruled off limits. The universality of theology's responsibility is based upon the unity of the Biblical
God as creator and redeemer of the world.

Theology has the task of seeing the connection between
the acts of God that the Bible reports and the events that
make up the history of the church and the world. "This
will mean speaking of the Biblical God as the one and true
God only in relation to universal history as the ultimate
horizon of reality. Universal history can also bridge over
the distance between the time of Jesus' earthly appearance
and the twentieth century, and thus make possible a solu-

tion of the hermeneutical problem."[23] A theology faithful to Scripture is led by the Biblical proclamation of God into an understanding of the world as history. What has happened since the death of the last apostle and the close of the Biblical canon has significance for theology.

For Pannenberg, hermeneutics cannot be abstracted out of the all-embracing theology of history which properly locates our contemporary situation in relation to the primitive Christian tradition. The hermeneutical gap is bridged by the continuing history of God's unfolding plan for the world. The church and its tradition have a structural significance in a hermeneutic of universal history. From the Protestant side this would seem to call for a rethinking of the relation between Scripture and tradition, with special reference to the *sola scriptura* principle and the hermeneutical value of creeds and confessions.

SCRIPTURE AND THE TRADITION

The ecumenical dialogue has forced Protestants and Roman Catholics to reconsider the images they have of each other—and of themselves. The high regard in which Protestants have held the Bible has been joined with an antithetical attitude toward the tradition of the church, its creeds and confessions. Roman Catholics have often reacted by deflating the significance of the Scriptures and inflating the value of their own traditions. At no point has there been more wrongheadedness and misunderstanding on both sides than on the question of the relation between Scripture and church tradition. The ecumenical dialogue provides the context in which needed changes can occur.

Developments within modern Roman Catholic theology have tended toward an accommodation of the Scripture principle as a hermeneutical control and critique of traditions in the church. Even the Reformation formula *sola scriptura* can be accepted in a Catholic sense. This principle emphasizes the sole sufficiency of Scripture with respect to the content of revelation. All the revelation is contained in Holy Scripture, meaning that post-Biblical tradition cannot be a source of additional revelation. To be sure, tradition also contains all the revelation, but only so far as it is derived from the Scriptural source. This is the view that progressive Roman Catholic theologians hold, in open conflict with the traditional, conservative position found in manuals of dogmatic theology written since the Council of Trent. This conservative position has been teaching that there are two sources of the whole revelation of God, part of it contained in Scripture and part in tradition. This theory conveniently makes room for all those Roman Catholic dogmas (mariological, papal, sacramental) for which not only Protestant but also Catholic exegetes find little or no support in Scripture. If the progressive view becomes ascendant and normative, Catholic Biblical scholars will be onstage to demonstrate how the authoritative dogmas in the tradition are a legitimate interpretation of the Scriptural revelation. Of course, the hermeneutical significance of the tradition is not renounced by the new Catholic theology of Scripture. The tradition of the Roman Church still serves as a bridge between the past revelatory event and the present situation, but now, at least in principle, it is a bridge that must rest on the solid foundations of Scripture.

The tension between the conservative and progressive theories on Scripture and tradition in Roman Catholicism is paralleled by a similar tension within Protestantism. The tension is characterized by a negative or positive attitude toward tradition as a hermeneutical guideline in Biblical interpretation. Radical Protestant theology regards tradition as so much rubble and deadweight which must be cleared away to get back to the gospel in Scripture. The opposing view, which we might call evangelical catholic theology, for lack of a better term, recognizes the ambiguity of tradition and its subordination to Scripture, yet places a high value on its power to mediate the fuller implications of the gospel, as the church under the guidance of the Holy Spirit has come to know them. The gulf between the Protestant radicals and evangelical catholics is clearly exhibited in their disagreement on the meaning of the sixteenth-century Reformation. The former sees the Reformation as a complete break with the catholic tradition, that is, as constitutive of a new beginning on the basis of Scripture alone (*sola scriptura*) as interpreted exclusively in the light of the principle of justification by faith alone (*sola fide*). The evangelical catholic view sees the Reformation as an important correction of the tradition, and in many ways, a continuation of the truly catholic heritage. This would seem to be the way the Reformers understood their own role. The very fact that the confessional writings of the Lutheran Church begin with an acceptance of the three great ecumenical creeds (Apostles', Nicene, Athanasian) underscores the intention of the Reformers to retain continuity with the entire catholic tradition, removing or correcting only those doctrinal or institutional developments incompatible with the gospel of Christ.

Gerhard Ebeling and Ernst Käsemann may be taken as representatives of a radical Protestant position that goes so far to expunge all catholic elements that only a torso of the historic Reformation theology is left intact. Typical of a broad Protestant mentality, Ebeling contrasts the

Protestant hermeneutical principle of the Word alone to the Catholic system of "Sacramental actualization."[24] We are asked to choose between a rather stark either/or: either the event of revelation is actualized today via the exposition of Scripture or via the Sacrament. Ebeling sees the Reformation as a revolution in hermeneutical method destroying all bridges between revelation and the present except the act of interpreting the Scriptures. In one great sweeping reductionist statement, Ebeling defines church history as the history of the interpretation of Scripture[25] —which it is, to be sure, but also more than that. One could scarcely object to Ebeling's laying great store by the Reformation principles of the Word alone, *sola fide, sola gratia;* but rather than interpreting the *sola* in a corrective sense, he makes it constitutive, isolating it and setting it against the catholic tradition of the church. An example of this is Ebeling's idea that the *sola fide* of the Reformation is at bottom an anti-Sacramental principle.[26] Protestantism is a church of the Word versus Catholicism as a church of Sacraments. Protestants who are evangelical catholics would not think of juxtaposing the Word to the Sacraments.

What role does the reality of the church and its tradition play in a Protestant hermeneutic that seeks to eradicate all so-called catholic elements as regulative in Biblical interpretation? At the Roman Catholic–Protestant Colloquium held at Harvard University in March, 1963, James M. Robinson defined the hermeneutical principle of Protestantism as the interpretation of Scripture in contrast to the Roman Catholic position which sees the councils of the church hierarchy as the definitive hermeneutical event.[27] Is such a simplistic juxtaposition of Scripture interpretation and church council really tenable for Protestants who view the Reformation as corrective rather than constitutive? Church councils are not to be a substitute for the interpretation of Scripture, but rather the means by which a contemporary actualization of the meaning of Biblical revelation might occur for the church. The fact that the conciliar movement suffered a false (papal and hierarchical) development within Roman Catholicism is no sufficient reason for Protestants to make a virtue of their own structural deficiency in this respect. If the interpretation of Scripture is the Protestant hermeneutical principle, *whose* interpretation amidst the plethora of doctrinal and exegetical opinions should be accepted as binding for church praxis in a given historical situation? At least Roman Catholics involved in the ecumenical dialogue are (rightly) not impressed by the Protestant answer to the hermeneutical question which finally condemns each exegete to serve as his own pope. There is a structural problem within Protestantism that is not solved by reiterating a thousand times that *sola scriptura* is the hermeneutical principle of Protestantism. There must be concrete structures within the church through which the hermeneutical process takes place from day to day. In Protestantism, the structures have become shadowy, if not invisible. In Roman Catholicism they have become overdeveloped and divinized. The response of the Reformation to the Romanization of the church was not to dismantle but to disencumber the structures of the church. Why, even the papacy was acceptable to the Reformers, but not all its actions and pretentious claims.

Once Protestant theologians set out to de-catholicize the faith, they find to their chagrin that they must carve out a large part of the New Testament. A hermeneutic of the Word alone, understood now exclusively as the gospel of justification by faith alone, will have to peel away layers of church tradition also within the New Testament. Ernst Käsemann has published his exegetical results showing that "early Catholicism" can be found already in the New Testament.[28] The fall of the church away from its pure apostolic origins into Catholicism did not happen after the fifth century, as the Reformation fathers expressed by their idea of a consensus during the first five centuries (*consensus quinquesaecularis*), nor did it happen during the second century by way of the "Hellenization of Christianity," as Adolf von Harnack believed, but, according to Ernst Käsemann, portions of Scripture, such as the pastoral epistles and Luke-Acts, provide ample evidence of an early Catholic development. By "early Catholicism," Käsemann has in mind the development of congregational order, church offices, the distinction between clerics and lay persons, the principles of ordination, succession, tradition, doctrine, and law. To these structures, Käsemann contrasts a picture of primitive Christianity ruled by the Spirit and endowed with the various "charismata."

The distinction between primitive Christianity and early Catholicism within the New Testament is so great that we are forced, Käsemann believes, to pay our money and take our choice. In a provocative essay, Käsemann has argued that the New Testament canon as a whole does not provide the basis for the unity of the church, but instead for a plurality of contradictory confessions. Käsemann's own words are: "The time when it was possible to set up Scripture in its totality in opposition to Catholicism has gone beyond recall. Protestantism today can no longer employ the so-called Formal Principle without rendering itself unworthy of credence in the eyes of historical analysis."[29] In Käsemann's opinion this means that the Protestant theologian must choose between that in the New Testament which found its flowering in the Reformation period or that which developed into later Catholicism. Otherwise stated, the decision is between the authentic gospel of the justification of the sinner, on the one hand, and the ordered institutionalization of the church as a social, corporate reality living in history, on the other hand. Then not the whole New Testament in its perplexing diversity is the canon for the church; but only a part of the New Testament, a "canon within the canon," that part which expresses the pure gospel, can be decisive for the Protestant confession.

Käsemann understands his own position as rigorously Lutheran. His is a hermeneutic of the word of justification by faith alone apart from the works of the church. For that which pertains to the *esse* of the church in the New Testament has been labeled "early Catholicism" and dismissed as sub- or anti-evangelical. By reminding us of the doctrinal excesses in later Roman Catholicism, he seeks to frighten us away from the full New Testament revelation of the catholicity of the church which, for us at least — and the Reformers — does not stand in antithesis to the gospel of the justification of the sinner. Soteriology and ecclesiology are two foci in an ellipse.

While we agree with Käsemann that the message of God's justification of the sinful and the ungodly is the heart of the New Testament, it does not stand isolable from the rest of the traditions of apostolic witness. It must also be said that Käsemann can offer no exegetically valid basis for his selection of one segment of the New Testament; the selection is made from an a priori dogmatic point of view; and only that in the New Testament which reflects his prior decision may be called the authentic apostolic gospel. Ecumenically Käsemann's position is manifestly untenable. In saying to Roman Catholic theology that the Protestant faith is founded upon only a part of the New Testament, it admits to having made an arbitrary choice against the church universal. This makes the ecumenical dialogue with Protestants too easy for Roman Catholics.[30] They do not even have to take such a position seriously, for it stands not only without the tradition of the universal church but also on only a partial fragment of the New Testament.

DOGMA AND LITURGY

The various hermeneutical proposals that we have cited all seek to leap over the historically continuous tradition of the church into a direct confrontation with Scripture on the strength of a single all-determinative category. The psychological hermeneutics of Schleiermacher and Dilthey, the existentialist hermeneutics of Bultmann, the linguistic hermeneutics of Ebeling and Fuchs offer no constitutive and positively significant place to the tradition of the church. Therefore, they cannot actually explain how the event of revelation attested to in Scripture becomes known and experienced as a living reality for us now. In our own conception the task of hermeneutics is twofold: (1) to describe the actual way by which contemporary believers are brought into an understanding relation to the Biblical message, and (2) to facilitate a full hearing of the *total* Biblical message. Käsemann's principle of justification, as we saw, was applied in such a way that it listened to only part of the total Biblical tradition. As a hermeneutical principle it then becomes self-refuting. But it need not be so, if the principle is not used reductionistically in relation to the Scriptures and polemically in relation to the tradition.

The tradition of the church provides in its creeds and confessions hermeneutical guidelines to its Biblical exegetes. The tradition itself is our link with the past. No hermeneutical access to the Scriptures as past historical documents is feasible except through the tradition. There is no way around the tradition. The tradition, however, is no monolith. It contains a variability of beliefs and a profusion of highly disharmonious doctrines. But such contradictions should not blind our eyes to the possibility of a central stream in the church's tradition with certain well-placed landmarks. These landmarks are the important creeds and confessions of the church. Besides discontinuities in the tradition of the church, there is continuity in creedal confession. Within Protestant theology we have witnessed a return to an appreciation of the hermeneutical function of dogma within an evangelical framework. In the nineteenth century, and certainly still in liberal Protestantism today, dogma was considered the badge of Catholicism. Wilhelm Herrmann and Adolf von Harnack could understand dogma only in its medieval Roman Catholic sense as a doctrinal law (*Lehrgesetz*) binding upon all in Christendom. The German periodical entitled *Kerygma and Dogma* was founded after World War II as a Protestant affirmation of the essential connection of dogma with kerygma. The hermeneutics of Bultmann's kerygmatic theology perpetuated the nineteenth-century neo-Protestant rejection of dogma. Now a countermovement began to express that dogma is important also for Protestants in the twentieth century. But for them dogma is not revealed truth, as it is for Roman Catholics, but a concentrated summary of the history of revelation composed by the church for hermeneutical reasons, that is, as aids in the reading and understanding of Scripture.

The Protestant recovery of the significance of dogma is

clearly exhibited by Karl Barth's voluminous *Church Dogmatics*. Barth defines dogma as the proclamation of the church, so far as it really agrees with the Bible as the Word of God.[31] Dogma is not the Word of God itself; it is not to be identified with the revelation as such. Rather, it is the answer of the church to the revelation; it is the echo of the Word of God in the church. It is the church's formulation of the truth of Holy Scripture as the church believes, teaches, and confesses this truth in various historical situations. The confessions of the church stand *under* the Scriptures. They do not intend to convey any revelation not already contained in Scripture. On the other hand, the confessions do stand *before* the Scriptures. They are closer to us than the Scriptures themselves. It is an undeniable and hermeneutically significant fact that each one learns the credo of the church before he reads the Scriptures. The credo of the church informs one's pre-understanding as one critically examines the Scriptural witness. The church's definitive confessions possess hermeneutical significance because they act like a signpost or a compass. They point beyond themselves to the saving revelation in Christ and to the main events and authoritative interpretations of those events in holy history. The Biblical exegete is offered, as it were, a map for his exegetical explorations through the Scriptures. He is told that this map has been used before, and has proven helpful to generations before him. It goes without saying that he in turn is asked to check up on the map, to see if it conforms to his actual findings. The narrow confessionalist is one who is satisfied to put the map in his pocket, and absentmindedly forgets to make the trip. The anticonfessionalist is one who sets off on the trip without taking any map along, or takes along a map which he arbitrarily dreamed up. The former sees the confessions as an end in themselves, falling into idolatry, the latter fails to see them as a means to an end, thus being guilty of iconoclasm.

The hermeneutical relevance of the traditional creeds of the church is by no means unconditional. As the words of Scripture itself, the past confessional recitations of the church may be only a "dead letter which kills." But they may also be living expressions of the continuity of the faith of the church catholic, as the Spirit breathes new life into the classic words and phrases within the community gathered in the name of the crucified and risen Lord. Without the active, inner witness of the Holy Spirit within the community of faith and worship, the tradition of the church would only be a crushing burden to be cast off. Anticonfessional liberalism is invariably a reaction against doctrinal legalism and ecclesiastical authoritarianism. The Spirit, however, does not work in a vacuum. The Spirit actualizes the redeeming presence of Christ through the tradition (Scriptures and church) which transmits the past memories and hopes of the people of God. It is finally the Spirit, and no immanental control by the church over the Word, who "merges the horizons" of the Biblical text and contemporary existence; it is the Spirit who makes the earthen vessels transmitters of heavenly treasures; it is the Spirit who spans the wide chasm of the centuries between Biblical *Heilsgeschichte* and present-day history. In the last analysis, a hermeneutic without the Pentecostal principle is a key that cannot unlock the mystery of God's revelation in Scripture.

The life situation in which the Spirit brings to remembrance today all that God has done for his people and mankind yesterday is the worship of the gathered community. Through Word and Sacrament, through hymn and prayer, the body with all its members enjoys the living presence of Christ its head through the Spirit. The Spirit uses liturgy as a means of transmitting the tradition of witness to Jesus Christ. Therefore, liturgy is an essential hermeneutical link between the past and the present. Like the dogma of the church, liturgy is a compressed form of tradition bearing the testimonies of the people of God to the history of salvation. The term "liturgy" comes from two Greek words, *laos* and *ergon,* meaning "people" and "work." Liturgy is the work of the people of God. Liturgy is dramatic; the word "drama" means "a thing that is done." Liturgy is a dramatic representation of the mighty saving acts of God in history. The history of God with his people is rehearsed, memories are refreshed, hopes are spawned in the context of worship. In worship the benefits of the past become presently actualized and the future preactualized in the Sacrament of Christ's real presence. Holy Communion, for example, is experienced as a foretaste of the heavenly banquet that Christ will host in the age that is coming.

Bishop John A. T. Robinson in his finest book, *Liturgy Coming to Life,* combats the notion that worship is an introverted activity of the church. On the contrary, there is a dynamic connection between liturgy and life. The liturgy of Holy Communion is the gospel in action, the "focus, the power-house, . . . the 'hot spot' of the church's whole existence."[32] Because Christ who exists for the world is active in the liturgy of Holy Communion, Robinson can speak of Communion as "social dynamite"[33]; it is the shrewdest political thing the church can do. Then he shows the inner connection between liturgy and the present social, political, and economic problems that speak to the conscience of the church. The hermeneutical bearing of this insight is inescapable. The Bible is the book of the church which she reads and expounds as an assembly of worshipers. The Bible can be *read* under any presuppositions; it can be *understood* only by the church as the charter of her existence. The act of understanding occurs as a miracle in the context of worship.

Our purpose in discussing the hermeneutical relevance of the tradition of the church, its dogma and liturgy, is to enlarge the framework within which the current debate on hermeneutics is taking place. The twin phenomena of the critical-historical method and existentialist (or linguistic) philosophy have recently taken command, in imperialistic fashion, of the hermeneutical concern. Historical and traditional links of the hermeneutical chain that keep us in living contact with God's work of redemption in the Old and New Testaments have dropped out of sight. A hermeneutic of the Word and the church will look beyond the individualistic limitations of existentialism to the corporate structures (such as dogma and liturgy) which mediate the reality and meaning of redemption through the changing times and situations of the history of God's people.

CHAPTER VII

Eschatology and History

TYPES OF ESCHATOLOGY

One of the most significant events in modern Protestant theology was the discovery of the dominance of eschatology in the teaching of Jesus and primitive Christianity. The effects of this discovery were far-reaching. First of all, it pulled the rug out from under the synthesis of Christianity and culture which nineteenth-century theologians had achieved. The basis of this synthesis had been the idea of the Kingdom of God defined by Kant and Ritschl as an ethical commonwealth gradually coming to perfection in history through love and moral actions. The Kingdom was coming through the progressive moral, spiritual development of mankind. The epoch-making book of Johannes Weiss on *The Preaching of Jesus Concerning the Kingdom of God*[1] and Albert Schweitzer's book on *The Quest of the Historical Jesus* had the combined effect of shattering the pillar on which liberal Christianity stood. They demonstrated that the Kingdom of God in Jesus' preaching was not a new order which men could build in partnership with God; rather, it was a reality breaking in from above as a great crisis and act of renewal solely worked by God.

A further consequence of the new emphasis on eschatology was the need to revise its place in dogmatic theology. Traditionally, eschatology was written as the last chapter in dogmatics, without explicit connection with what went before. It served more as an appendix to theology. Now it was seen that all theology must be penetrated by eschatology, for eschatology deals not only with "the last things" in the order of chronology but also with "the ultimate things" in an existential sense. While there is general agreement among scholars that eschatology cannot be a bloodless chapter tacked on to a theological system, a sort of speculative gazing into the future, there is lacking a consensus on several crucial points: (1) on the nature and development of eschatological thinking in the New Testament and (2) on how to translate the meaning of eschatology into categories somewhat congenial to the modern temper. How did Jesus and the early church think of the Kingdom of God? Was the Kingdom fully realized in the ministry and destiny of Jesus? Or was it inaugurated by Jesus and therefore now in the process of being realized? Or does the accent of the coming of the Kingdom lie in the future at the end of time? Other questions, too, insinuated themselves. Is there a blatant contradiction between the eschatological teaching of Jesus and that of the early church? Did the church have to revise its eschatological hopes as history rolled on and as the Parousia of Christ seemed to be indefinitely postponed? And, to mention another possibility, is not the entire framework and content of New Testament eschatology so utterly foreign to our modern way of thinking that we must simply reckon with the necessity of stripping it away altogether before we can find that which is permanently valid for Christianity? As we survey the history of eschatology in twentieth-century

Protestant theology, we will see all these questions debated and variously answered. Indeed, it is possible to delineate quite a variety of types of constructions on the problem of eschatology and history.

1. *Consistent eschatology.* This is the common label placed on the viewpoint advanced by Johannes Weiss and Albert Schweitzer and now currently represented by the extreme, liberal wing of Protestant theology in the writings of Martin Werner and Fritz Buri of Switzerland.[2] According to Schweitzer's school, Jesus' preaching of the Kingdom is thoroughly stamped by the traits of late Jewish apocalypticism. When Jesus preached "Repent, for the kingdom of God is at hand," he was announcing that in a very short time the Kingdom would be ushered in by a catastrophic judgment; also the first Christians believed that the end of the world was imminent. Everything in Jesus' ministry of word and deed can be explained in the light of his eschatological expectation. Even his decision to go to the cross was an attempt to trigger off the eschatological chain of events.

There are several noteworthy points in Schweitzer's portrayal. First, Schweitzer correctly saw that Jesus' eschatology was central, not peripheral, to his thinking. It could not be easily laid aside in favor of the simple ethic of the Sermon on the Mount. In fact, Jesus' ethical teachings, taken literally, make sense only as an "interim ethic," that is, as binding only during this short interval until the final in-breaking of the rule of God. They were not propounded on the assumption that the world would last for a long time to come. Secondly, scholars in general have confirmed Schweitzer's thesis that Jesus and the first Christians expected the end of history in *their* generation, and that the fact that this did not happen constituted a major theological problem for second and third generation Christians. Thirdly, Schweitzer and his followers, Werner and Buri, conclude that because the end did not come as expected, eschatology itself has been nullified by the fact of the ongoingness of history. Although eschatology formed the decisive core of Jesus' message, it is impossible to discover abiding meaning in it for our time. Eschatology is riveted to a world view that we have long ago outgrown. It has rightly been said that in Schweitzer we have "the anomaly of a scholar who does not belong to his own school of thought—not, that is to say, so far as the school would endeavor to identify its own teachings with those of the historic Jesus."[3] Schweitzer's own ethical mysticism, popularized in the slogan "reverence for life," at least has the merit of being unique among the liberal versions of Christianity in that it does not claim to have Jesus of Nazareth for its founder.

2. *Realized eschatology.* The name of C. H. Dodd is practically synonymous with the view that the *eschaton* was fully realized in the coming of Christ. Whereas Schweitzer and colleagues emphasized the strictly futuristic character of the Kingdom as preached by Jesus, denying altogether any present, realized aspects in Jesus' ministry, Dodd offers an equally consistent but opposing view that the Kingdom had already arrived in and with Jesus, denying or explaining away all future references. In announcing the Kingdom, Jesus was not predicting what was going to happen, however soon, but was actually introducing the Kingdom then and there. "The kingdom of God is in the midst of you." (Luke 17:21.)

Dodd accepts Schweitzer's basic point that Jesus' ministry cannot be understood apart from eschatology, as most of the liberal nineteenth-century biographers of Jesus had tried to do. His quarrel with Schweitzer has chiefly to do with the time factor regarding the coming of the Kingdom in Jesus' preaching. The eschatology of Jesus does not point to an expected future but to a present reality, the dynamic eruption of God's sovereign rule in Jesus' ministry. The classic statement of Dodd's conception of realized eschatology was worked out in his book *The Parables of the Kingdom*. Here he convincingly defends his thesis that the crisis of the Kingdom is present in Jesus' own ministry, and men are confronted with the challenge to decide for or against it. The question other scholars have raised, with an eye to the truth in Schweitzer's futuristic emphasis, is whether the Kingdom is *wholly* realized in Jesus' ministry, leaving the future as a kind of meaningless epilogue to the present. Scholars who believe that Jesus taught both a present and a future aspect of the Kingdom view Dodd's dismissal of the future references as an exegetical *tour de force*. In Platonic fashion, Dodd interprets those sayings which refer to the future as pointing symbolically to a transcendent, spiritual world beyond time and space.

It is significant that, in later writings, Dodd modified his idea of realized escatology in conceding significance to the history that follows the Christ event.[4] The resurrection, Pentecost, and the missionary history of the church are not to be excluded as factors in the advent of the Kingdom. It would seem, then, that Dodd could go at least part way in accepting a revision of his scheme of realized eschatology advocated by scholars like Joachim Jeremias, Werner G. Kümmel, and Oscar Cullmann.[5] These scholars are grateful to both Schweitzer and Dodd for having stressed different but equally important aspects of eschatology. Jeremias has volunteered the expression *"sich reali-*

siernde Eschatologie" (eschatology in process of realization) to hold together both Schweitzer's emphasis on the future aspect and Dodd's counteremphasis on the present element.

3. Heilsgeschichte *eschatology.* The position of *Heilsgeschichte* theologians like Jeremias, Kümmel, and Cullmann, who combine the present and future elements in the teaching of Jesus about the Kingdom, has the distinct advantage of holding the tension between the "already" and the "not yet" in the drama of salvation. Moreover, this position closes the gap between Jesus' own eschatological outlook and the later working out of a theology of eschatological history in the early church. The early church remained basically faithful to the internal structure of Jesus' own eschatology which counts on a period of historical time running between the event of salvation in Jesus and a final eschatological event which signals the end of history —the Parousia. The period of church history is suspended in recollection of the past and anticipation of the future of Christ's coming.

The most widely known scheme of *Heilsgeschichte* eschatology is one sketched by Cullmann in *Christ and Time.* Cullmann sees history as a straight line running between the creation and the Parousia, intersected at the midpoint by the coming of Christ. He uses the vivid metaphor of the distinction between "D-day" and "V-day" to illustrate that in Jesus' cross and resurrection, the decisive battle of the war has already occurred, but the important mopping-up exercises must still go on until "Victory Day." The tension between the "already" and the "not yet" is preserved. In Cullmann's scheme, eschatology deals literally with the "last things" in the sense of linear, calendar time. Each day, every minute, brings the end of history a little closer. Eschatology is the closing chapter of time, the last act in the drama of sacred history.

It is not our intention to deal with the questionable features of Cullmann's outline of the primitive Christian understanding of time and history. Were we to do that, his quantitative view of eternity as endless time would come up for particular criticism.[6] Also his tendency to flatten out the evidence in the Bible to fit a neat geometrically arranged scheme of historical interpretation has been severely challenged.[7] Yet, it cannot be denied that Cullmann's idea of *Heilsgeschichte* has stubbornly resisted the tendency of existentialist mysticism to dissolve the future horizon of Christian eschatology into the existential futurity of each individual self in the moment of decision.

4. *Existentialist eschatology.* In the theology of Rudolf Bultmann, eschatology loses its reference to an objective future end of history which the New Testament depicts in the imagery of apocalyptic mythology. Instead, existential significance replaces temporal reference in the definition of eschatology. Any moment or situation in which I have to make an ultimately significant decision may be called eschatological. Eternal life is the life I receive now; judgment is the crisis in which I stand now; the end-time is the *kairos* in which the issue of life and death is being decided. To the eyes of faith any moment could be the fullness of time. The *eschaton* does not lie in the future of mankind's history but in the immediate future that impinges on the present moment of my existence, qualifying it in a meaningful way. The *eschaton* is the time God gives me as an opportunity to decide for authentic existence. The forgiveness of sins proclaimed through the kerygma is an eschatological event; existence in faith is eschatological existence. The word "eschatology" has ob-

viously undergone a drastic revision of meaning. The futuristic eschatology of the New Testament has been demythologized and transposed into categories defining the possibilities of human existence. Bultmann believes that Paul and John may be appealed to as precedents for doing just this.[8]

Bultmann's study of the letters of Paul convinces him that Paul actually operated with two conceptions of eschatology: the scheme of *Heilsgeschichte* which concerns itself with a history of redemption that will be consummated in the final drama of the Parousia of Christ, and the existentialist which stresses the fulfillment in the now, radically converting the past and the future into the present moment. Bultmann sees no way of maintaining both of Paul's two eschatological emphases; only the existentialist view is tenable today in the light of our contemporary knowledge of man and the world. Moreover, Bultmann believes that the existentialist view is distinctively Pauline and Christian. Paul's idea of *Heilsgeschichte* was merely taken over from apocalyptic Judaism and is not essential to his understanding of existence *coram deo* (before God). Thus, we see that the same motives that impelled Bultmann to discount the Old Testament as salvation history are now at work to eliminate the future stretch of history leading to the final consummation of God's plan of redemption for the world.

If Bultmann's radical conversion of eschatology into each existential encounter in the present time can be supported by one side—the mystical side—of Paul's theology, there is even more justification, he feels, for invoking the Gospel of John as substantiation for a thoroughgoing contemporizing of eschatology. Be it noted, however, that in order to appeal to John's Gospel in support of an existen-

tialist eschatology in which the temporal references to the
past and the future are both entirely collapsed into the
pregnant present, Bultmann assumes that all the passages
in our present Fourth Gospel that contain a temporal
eschatology have been added by a later churchly revision
and reworking of the original text of the Johannine author.
The original text is completely uninterested in the past
and the future; the idea of a cosmic drama at the end of
history is absent; there is nothing but the existential category of the present moment in which the events of judgment and mercy, faith and love, occur through the present
proclamation of the kerygma.

We could say that Bultmann operates with a radically
realized eschatology, on the basis of his interpretations of
Paul and John. However, for Bultmann, in distinction
from C. H. Dodd, eschatology is realized not in the ministry of the historical Jesus but in the proclamation of the
kerygma here and now. Actually Bultmann accepts the
theory of "consistent eschatology" of Weiss and Schweitzer
so far as the historical Jesus is concerned. Jesus really expected the end of all history in his own immediate future,
but later history proved that he was mistaken in this expectation. In the face of this embarrassment, Bultmann
has recourse to the unhistorical, existential eschatology of
Paul and John in which the historical Jesus, in Bultmann's
interpretation, possesses no decisive significance.

What makes Bultmann's thinking on eschatology most
bewildering is that he not only finds his existential view
of eschatology in Paul and John, but his own writings on
Jesus seem to suggest that beneath the apocalyptic features
of Jesus' preaching of the Kingdom, there lies a deep sub-
stratum of a purely existentialist understanding of eschatology, notably in the radicality of God's demands, the

centrality of decision, and the accent on the present as determinative of man's existence.[9] From an existentialist perspective the basic and deepest understanding of eschatology runs through Jesus, Paul, and John. The *Heilsgeschichte* type of eschatology may admittedly be found in the Synoptic Gospels, The Acts, Hebrews, and Pastoral Epistles, Revelation, in portions of Paul's Epistles, and in the churchly redaction of the Gospel of John. The existentialist and *Heilsgeschichte* types of eschatalogy are pitted against each other; the theologian chooses which he prefers by whatever criterion, be it what is "most relevant to the modern" or "most primitively Christian"; and inescapably the canon of the church and the content of the creed are pared down to a miserably meager minimum.

Bultmann's disciples have been busy modifying their master's existentialist view of history and eschatology. We have already noted in Chapter III how they lay greater stress on the significance of the historical Jesus for the kerygma and faith. What this means is that the dimension of the past on the continuum of history has been accorded a more decisive role in the event of salvation than Bultmann could consistently allow. Bornkamm's book *Jesus of Nazareth* shows that for him the Kingdom of God is already breaking into history in the ministry of Jesus. The other post-Bultmannians like Käsemann, Fuchs, Conzelmann, and Ebeling also move beyond a present-tense eschatology in which past history is relatively unimportant. But what about the future tense? At this point they are not equally zealous. When they speak of the future, they refer not to a temporal but an existential future, namely, the futurity of existence. While criticizing Bultmann for dissolving the past into the present and running the danger of a docetic elimination of the historical humanity of Jesus of Nazareth, they do not with equal sensitivity call into question Bultmann's dismantling of the future goal of history. The future these pupils of Bultmann have in mind is not the future Advent of Jesus Christ, the end of history, the final consummation of the cosmos, the fulfillment of the destiny of each individual person. In dependence on Heidegger's idea of time and history,[10] they see the category of the future as an attribute of human existence, therefore designating primarily possibilities of existential decision, but not as an attribute of the historical reality of the world in purposeful forward movement under God's directing control toward an ultimate *telos*.

To my knowledge, only Ernst Käsemann in the wider circle of Bultmannians has raised serious doubts about the adequacy of an existentialist demythologizing of the future point of reference in the early Christian theology of history. He has expressed these doubts in his startling thesis that "apocalypticism is . . . the mother of all Christian theology."[11] In the oldest Christian prophecy the Christ event does not signify the "end of history" but the beginning of a new, final period of history filled with hopes for the coming Parousia. It was precisely this future orientation which Bultmann was prepared to renounce as Jewish mythology and less than genuinely Christian. In commenting on the first Christian understanding of history that locates the goal of the history of salvation in the future Parousia of the Son of Man Jesus, Käsemann says: "The mythical character of this approach to history can hardly be denied. Yet it is doubtless too easy for this reason simply to replace it with the modern insight into the historicity of existence, which, in isolation, lets the connection of history collapse into a sequence of more or less unrelated situations, reduces God's future to man's futurity, understands the present primarily in terms of the requirement placed upon us and the past ultimately as the foil or model of the decision to be made by us. It is highly questionable how far such an ethical approach to history is able to preserve its eschatological character."[12]

Käsemann represents a new departure not only from Bultmann's existentialism but also from the linguistic hermeneutical position that Fuchs and Ebeling conceived of as one step beyond Bultmann. This new departure from within the Bultmann school has the possibility of merging with or at least reinforcing the proleptic eschatology of Wolfhart Pannenberg in which the end of history is both present and future: present in the resurrection of Jesus and future for the rest of humanity. Meanwhile Ernst Fuchs and Gerhard Ebeling wasted no time in publishing rejoinders to Käsemann's new interest in Jewish-Christian apocalypticism.[13] Fuchs fails to see any relevance for faith and preaching today in the early Christian expectation of a future end of history ushered in by the return of Christ, and Ebeling reminds us that since the Reformation the very word "apocalyptic" has aroused suspicions of heretical (sectarian) tendencies. Käsemann, in a reply to his critics, opens the breach still wider by marshaling further exegetical evidences for his rehabilitation of the theme of primitive Christian apocalypticism.[14] Where this will lead Käsemann's research in the long run and what theological consequences will be drawn from it by other theologians only the next decade of theology can tell. What is significant now is that apocalypticism as a theme of theology has been hoisted out of oblivion from the side of both the Old and New Testament disciplines, and has already found its way into systematic theology through Wolfhart Pannenberg's theology of universal history. Could it be that here we have a potential point of contact in ecumenical circles with those of the left-wing Reformation (Pentecostals, etc.) who have cultivated apocalyptic eschatology with as much zeal as it has been omitted by the more traditional denominations of Reformation descent? Could it be also that the so-called sects in their rather fantastic interpretations of contemporary and future world history have nevertheless borne witness to an intransigent concern of Christian faith for the present world order and for the outcome of mankind's history?

5. *Dialectical eschatology*. Without claiming to have exhausted the possibilities of a typological study of modern eschatology, we conclude with a brief delineation of the dialectical eschatology that came to the fore during the 1920's in the writings of theologians like Paul Althaus, Karl Barth, and Emil Brunner, and still survives in Paul Tillich's third volume of *Systematic Theology*. There is strong family resemblance between, for example, the dialectical eschatology of the early Barth (e.g., in his Romans Commentary) and Bultmann's existentialist eschatology. Yet it deserves to be treated separately as a distinctive type because its dominant motif is the dialectical relation between eternity and time, and, at least by intention, moves out from a transcendental, theocentric view of eternity rather than an existentialist, phenomenological view of time.

One of the great works of eschatology is Paul Althaus' *Die letzten Dinge* (1922). Only the first edition of this work follows the pattern of dialectical eschatology; the later editions reflect a development in Althaus' thinking away from German idealism, which conceived of eschatology in spatial terms "above and beyond history," and toward a Biblical realism which pictures eschatology in temporal terms as the end point in a history of redemption. The latest stage in his thinking can be said to have come full circle in espousing the *Heilsgeschichte* type of eschatology.[15] Karl Barth traveled much the same route, so that today he has largely overcome his earlier hostility to *Heilsgeschichte*.

In any case, Althaus and Barth in their earlier period shared a deep disinterest in the future end of history. Althaus conceded the usefulness of images about the final goal of history in the practical instruction of simple people. But really the "last things" are the "ultimate things" of life that have to do with conscience and not chronology. Each person and each generation is equidistant from eternity. Eschatology has nothing to do with the end of history, only with the eternal transcendental meaning of each moment in history. Eternity is supratemporal and therefore always contemporary. Nineteen centuries of church history have not brought us closer to the end of time; the end is the quality of eternity breaking in suddenly from above, bringing everything earthly and human under judgment. Weary of culture Protestantism and disenchanted with the liberal doctrine of progress, Barth and his friends heard the gospel in the austere message that God is in his eternal heaven, and man, a transitory creature of time, is on earth. There is no doubt that in this theology of crisis, profound and much-neglected elements of Biblical and Reformation Christianity were being recovered. The recovery, however, was only partial. Althaus and Barth were both mired in the very idealistic matrix of thinking which they struggled so hard to transcend. This was especially true of the dissolution of the real future of Christ and history in a dialectic of eternity and time.

The problem of eschatology is also conceived by Tillich in terms of the dialectic of eternity and time. The difference is chiefly that Tillich unfolds the dialectic in ontological categories, whereas Karl Barth uses more and more the traditional language of the Bible and ecclesiastical Christology. Both have tried to steer a middle course between the Platonic idea of eternity as timelessness and the naïve idea of eternity as endless time (Cullmann). "Eternity," says Tillich, "is the transcendent unity of the dissected moments of existential time."[16] Eternity does not negate time, but includes it while transcending it. In Tillich the dialectic keeps the temporal within the eternal; in Barth the dialectic breaks in half so that the eternal and temporal stand entirely outside each other. Tillich sees their difference in unity, Barth their difference in duality. Both, however, agree that eschatology is the problem of the right relation between eternity and time, and tend to stress the present tense as the bearer of eternal meaning (the *nunc aeternum*).[17] The future tense of eschatology never receives its due in a dialectical conceptuality. This is especially serious, as the future tense is essential to the language of promise and fulfillment, the language of hope and expectancy, the language appropriate to us as a *communio viatorum* who "groan inwardly as we wait for adoption as sons, the redemption of our bodies" (Rom. 8:23). Eschatology that does not focus on the future yet to happen does not give expression to the *hope* of faith.

√ THE HOPE OF HISTORY

In 1954, the Second Assembly of the World Council of Churches met in Evanston, Illinois, under the banner "Christ the Hope of the World!" The most memorable event of that meeting was the confrontation of two theological viewpoints. Dr. Edmund Schlink, of Heidelberg, and Dr. Robert L. Calhoun, of Yale, were billed by the press as the spokesmen for the clash between a pessimistic European eschatology of crisis and an optimistic American doctrine of progress in history.[18] The deep split did not develop as those looking for a good scrap had hoped. Schlink's eschatology did not abandon hope for the world and Calhoun's understanding of history reckoned with the powers of evil and the judgment of God. Both were united in a ringing affirmation of Christ as the ultimate hope of mankind. Evanston's message of hope was proclaimed to the churches. A number of theologians produced special monographs on "the Christian hope."[19] That was slightly over a decade ago. Since then, Western Christendom in general has been skidding into an attitude of hopelessness. Doubt and despair are the deadliest sins against hope.

In the last decade the so-called vanguard voices in the church have coined a spate of slogans symptomatic of these deadly sins, resulting in a loss of self-identity on the part of the church and her theologians. This is the decade in which Bonhoeffer's "religionless Christianity" rang a bell, when theologians proclaimed "the death of God" and believed they could translate the gospel into completely secular categories, when the church was challenged to prove her relevance by becoming a kind of social welfare agency, and the secular city was celebrated as modern man's dream of the Kingdom of God.

From within, the church is undergoing a deep crisis of faith, threatened by a loss of continuity with her past and by an aborted consciousness of mission and destiny in the world. On the outside we are witnessing the resurgence of rival hopes that buoy men up with a sense of universal purpose and destiny. Much of the real Christian eschatology has been drained out of Christianity and now exists in heretical form in Communism. World history has a meaning and a goal in Marxism. It is difficult to imagine anything more irrelevant to proclaim to men of our time than a Christian message which retreats from the arena of universal history into the private sphere of existential decisions.

At the end of his Gifford Lectures on *History and Eschatology,* Bultmann offers this counsel to the modern man searching for an answer to the question of meaning in history: "We have seen that man cannot answer this question as the question of the meaning in history in its totality. For man does not stand outside history. But now we can say: *the meaning in history lies always in the present,* and when the present is conceived as the eschatological present by Christian faith the meaning in history is realized. Man who complains: 'I cannot see meaning in history, and therefore my life, interwoven in history, is meaningless,' is to be admonished: Do not look around yourself into universal history; you must look into your own personal history. Always in your present lies the meaning in history, and you cannot see it as a spectator, but only in your responsible decisions. In every moment slumbers the possibility of being the eschatological moment. You must awaken it."[20]

The withdrawal of the Christian faith from the sphere of universal history makes the appeal of the gospel of Communism all the greater and understandable. The strength of a gospel is derived from the hopes it inspires in the hearts of men. But what is the hope that the Christian faith holds forth for mankind in an age of universal history? Certainly it is something more than a gospel of individual salvation *hic et nunc.*

One of the finest books in theology written in recent years is Jürgen Moltmann's *Theology of Hope* (1965), a study of the foundations and implications of a Christian eschatology. When German theologians are asked what is new in theology since Barth and Bultmann besides Ebeling and Pannenberg, they point to Jürgen Moltmann. One of the exciting things about this book is the underlying dialogue it engages in with a two-volume work written by a Marxist, Ernst Bloch, on the principle of hope (*Das Prinzip Hoffnung*). Bloch, of course, is an atheist, but one of those atheists who takes the trouble to try to understand the Bible and Christian language about God.[21] In removing the hypothesis of God, Bloch tries to retain what it stood for, namely, an eschatology of hope turned toward the future. Moltmann is not attracted to Bloch's atheistic interpretation of religion, but rebaptizes the originally Christian eschatological dynamic of his philosophy of hope. Moltmann's project is to forge a language of hope that corresponds not to the category of the Greek *logos* but to the Biblical category of promise. Actually, there can be no eschato-*logy*, for the Greek term *logos* brings to expression a reality that is always there and has only to be grasped by our intellect. *Logos* is at home in the static world of Parmenides' being. In contrast, the category of promise suggests a future in which something really new happens. Christian eschatology speaks of the specific future of Jesus Christ on the basis of the reality of his resurrection; the future will bring not only a revelation of what already exists hiddenly, nor a repetition of what has previously happened, but something really new—the fulfillment of the promise of righteousness for all, the realization of the resurrection of all the dead, and the universal acknowledgment of Jesus Christ as Lord over all.

The theme of eschatology as the future of Jesus Christ has also been expounded by other younger dogmaticians: Heinrich Ott, of Basel, and Walter Kreck, of Bonn.[22] As pupils of Karl Barth they reflect his Christocentric emphasis; yet they also acknowledge the legitimacy of Bultmann's concern to make all theological statements existentially relevant. At the crucial point they transcend their teachers—neither Barth nor Bultmann adequately maintain the eschatological tension. The "not yet" is too easily swallowed up by the "already." The future tends to be preempted (we could also say preemptied) by the present. Eschatology defines the reality of Christ not only axiologically as Bultmann does, not only transcendentally as the dialectical theologians did, but also in terms of temporal futurity and finality as Moltmann, Ott, and Kreck do. The temporal dimension of finality cannot be excluded, for that would be to deny the relation of the sovereign Lord to the future of history. As the Alpha and Omega, Christ is Lord also over the future end of personal existence, world history, and cosmic evolution.

We would suggest, on the basis of our discussion, several valid criteria for making appropriate eschatological statements. Eschatological statements must be *existentially relevant,* i.e., they must concern man's existence, his being and acting, his thinking and hoping. This should not be understood in a subjectivistic sense, as if they are merely statements *about* existence or reducible to existential self-understanding, as tends to happen in Bultmann's demythologizing interpretation.

Eschatological statements must be controlled by the *kerygma deriving from the Scriptures,* i.e., they must be essential to the preaching of the church today as the church stands under the authority of the Word of Holy Scripture. This should not be taken in a Biblicistic sense, as if the church should repeat everything in Biblical eschatology merely because "the Bible tells me so." The church must preach in a responsible way, willing to bear witness to what she has really heard from the Scriptures as God's Word concerning the future of history in Jesus Christ.

Eschatological statements must be *Christological,* i.e., centered in Christ as the *eschaton.* Any non-Christological interpretation of history is anachronistic, for it proceeds as if Christ had not happened in history, as if he is not the yesterday, today, and tomorrow of the history of everyman and the world.

Finally, eschatological statements must be *futuristic,* i.e., related not only to the depth dimension of present existence in relation to the eternal. The present without its past and future is fleeting and meaningless. Eschatology must point out the realm of the future hope beyond death, springing from the victory of God in the resurrection of Jesus.

Notes

Notes

Chapter I
The Idea of Revelation Through History

1. Paul Althaus, "Die Inflation des Begriffs der Offenbarung in der gegenwärtigen Theologie," *Zeitschrift für systematische Theologie,* 18 (1941), 134–149.

2. Paul Tillich, *Systematic Theology* (The University of Chicago Press, 1951), Vol. I, p. 67.

3. Gustaf Wingren, *Theology in Conflict,* tr. by Eric H. Wahlstrom (Muhlenberg Press, 1958). The polemics are directed also against Rudolf Bultmann and Anders Nygren.

4. James Barr, "Revelation Through History in the Old Testament and in Modern Theology," *Interpretation,* 17 (1963), 193–205.

5. *Ibid.,* p. 197.

6. Immanuel Kant, *Religion Within the Limits of Reason Alone,* tr. by T. M. Greene and H. H. Hudson (Harper & Brothers, 1960), p. 143.

7. Of the leading contemporary theologians Paul Tillich has the most comprehensive understanding of the media of revelation. He cites nature, history, groups, individuals, and the word. *Systematic Theology,* Vol. I, pp. 118–126.

8. Friedrich Schleiermacher, *The Christian Faith,* tr. by H. R. Mackintosh and J. S. Stewart (Edinburgh: T. & T. Clark, 1928), p. 50.

9. Quoted from Hermann Diem, *Dogmatics,* tr. by Harold Knight (Edinburgh: Oliver & Boyd, Ltd., 1959), p. 6.

10. *Revolutionary Theology in the Making: Barth-Thurney-sen Correspondence, 1914–1925*, tr. by James D. Smart (John Knox Press, 1964), p. 36.

11. Among them are Ulrich Wilckens, Dietrich Roessler, Klaus Koch, Rolf Rendtorff, Trutz Rendtorff, and M. Elze.

12. In the introductory chapter of the revised edition of his book *Christ and Time*, Cullmann rejoices that the theological climate has changed so that perhaps now his book can be better understood and appreciated. He points to W. Pannenberg and his friends as signs of a shift in the theological atmosphere.

13. Paul Althaus, *Fact and Faith in the Kerygma of Today*, tr. by David Cairns (Muhlenberg Press, 1959).

14. *Offenbarung als Geschichte*, ed. by Wolfhart Pannenberg *et al.*, 2d ed. (Göttingen: Vandenhoek & Ruprecht, 1963). The first edition was issued in 1961.

15. Friedrich Gogarten, *Demythologizing and History*, tr. by N. H. Smith (London: SCM Press, Ltd., 1955), Chapter VII.

16. Wolfhart Pannenberg, "Redemptive Event and History," *Essays on Old Testament Hermeneutics*, ed. by Claus Westermann, tr. by James Luther Mays (John Knox Press, 1964), pp. 314–315.

17. Pannenberg, *Offenbarung als Geschichte*, pp. 91–114.

18. E.g., Lothar Steiger, "Offenbarungsgeschichte und theologische Vernunft," *Zeitschrift für Theologie und Kirche*, 59 (1962), 93.

19. Quoted from Karl Barth, *Protestant Thought: From Rousseau to Ritschl*, tr. by Brian Cozens (Harper & Brothers, 1959), p. 137.

20. Pannenberg's interpretation of Hegel's significance for theology may be found in his essay, "Was ist Wahrheit?" in *Vom Herrengeheimnis der Wahrheit*, Festschrift für Heinrich Vogel, ed. by Kurt Scharf (Berlin: Lattner-Verlag, 1962), pp. 214–239.

21. In a book dedicated to their teacher von Rad, a number of theologians in Pannenberg's circle have written chapters that show their indebtedness to him, but also how they are going beyond him to demonstrate the fundamental thesis that the Old Testament is a "book of history." *Studien zur Theologie der alttestamentlichen Überlieferungen*, ed. by Rolf Rendtorff and Klaus Koch (Verlag der Buchhandlung des Erziehungsvereins Neukirchen Kreis Moers), 1961.

CHAPTER II
THEOLOGY AND THE HISTORICAL-CRITICAL METHOD

1. Paul Tillich, *Systematic Theology* (The University of Chicago Press, 1957), Vol. II, p. 107.

2. Most notably Heinrich Schlier, a Bultmannian who converted to the Roman Catholic Church. See the sections on Heinrich Schlier's conception of church and dogma in Hermann Diem's *Dogmatics,* pp. 41–52, 107–111.

3. David Hume, *An Enquiry Concerning Human Understanding,* Sec. VIII, Part I. (Italics mine.)

4. Gerhard Ebeling, *Word and Faith,* tr. by James W. Leitch (Fortress Press, 1963).

5. Erwin Reisner, "Hermeneutik und historische Vernunft," *Zeitschrift für Theologie und Kirche,* 49 (1952), 223–237.

6. James Robinson, *A New Quest of the Historical Jesus* (London: SCM Press, Ltd., 1959), p. 28.

7. Heinrich Ott, "The Historical Jesus and the Ontology of History," *The Historical Jesus and the Kerygmatic Christ,* tr. and ed. by Carl E. Braaten and Roy A. Harrisville (Abingdon Press, 1964), p. 166.

8. See especially Gerhard Ebeling, *Theologie und Verkündigung* (Tübingen: J. C. B. Mohr, 1962).

9. Gerhard Ebeling, "The Significance of the Critical Historical Method," *Word and Faith,* pp. 58–59.

10. Wolfhart Pannenberg, "Heilsgeschehen und Geschichte," *Kerygma und Dogma,* 5 (1959), 259–261.

11. This abbreviated summary of Pannenberg's view of the anthropocentrism of historical criticism and its principle of analogy is based on the second part of his article "Heilsgeschehen und Geschichte," *loc. cit.* The first part has been translated into English by Shirley Guthrie and appears in *Essays on Old Testament Hermeneutics,* ed. by Claus Westermann (John Knox Press, 1964).

12. Rudolf Bultmann, "Is Exegesis Without Presuppositions Possible?" *Existence and Faith,* ed. by Schubert Ogden (Meridian Books, 1960), pp. 291–292.

13. Pannenberg, "Heilsgeschehen und Geschichte," *loc. cit.,* 266–267.

14. Richard R. Niebuhr, *Resurrection and Historical Reason* (Charles Scribner's Sons, 1957).

15. Alan Richardson, *History Sacred and Profane* (The Westminster Press, 1964), pp. 46–47.

16. Gerhard Ebeling, "The 'Non-religious Interpretation of Biblical Concepts,' " *Word and Faith*, p. 125.

17. The "as if" theory of Hans Vaihinger is an extreme form of neo-Kantianism which holds that an idea that is theoretically untrue may still have tremendous practical value. Ideas that prove to have practical value may be accepted "as if" they are true, even though we know they are fictions. The parallel between this "as if" philosophy and certain types of modern apologetics for religion is conspicuously striking.

18. Paul Althaus, "Offenbarung als Geschichte und Glaube: Bemerkungen zu Wolfhart Pannenbergs Begriff der Offenbarung," *Theologische Literaturzeitung*, 87 (1962), 321–330.

19. On the functions of the kerygma, see Pannenberg, *Offenbarung als Geschichte*, pp. 112–114.

20. Wolfhart Pannenberg, "Einsicht und Glaube: Antwort an Paul Althaus," *Theologische Literaturzeitung*, 88 (1963), 81–92.

21. For a more complete presentation of Pannenberg's views on revelation and reason see my article "The New Controversy on Revelation: Pannenberg and His Critics," *The Journal of Religion*, Vol. XLV, No. 3 (July, 1965).

CHAPTER III

OUR KNOWLEDGE OF THE HISTORICAL JESUS

1. Albert Schweitzer, *The Quest of the Historical Jesus* (The Macmillan Company, 1961), pp. 3–4.

2. Cf. Gunther Backhaus, *Kerygma und Mythos bei David Friedrich Strauss und Rudolf Bultmann* (Hamburg: Herbert Reich Evangelischer Verlag, 1956).

3. Henry J. Cadbury wrote a book by this title, showing how the modern religious interests of the scholars tend to distort their perception of the gospel materials. *The Peril of Modernizing Jesus* (The Macmillan Company, 1937).

4. Rudolf Bultmann, *Jesus and the Word*, tr. by Louise P. Smith and Ermine H. Lantero (Charles Scribner's Sons, 1934), p. 9.

5. Emil Brunner, *The Mediator*, tr. by Olive Wyon (The Westminster Press, 1947), pp. 186–187.

6. Paul Tillich, *Systematic Theology*, Vol. II, p. 102.

7. Karl Barth, *Church Dogmatics*, tr. by G. T. Thomson

and Harold Knight (Charles Scribner's Sons, 1956), Vol. I, Part 2, pp. 64–65.

8. Quoted from Hermann Diem, *Dogmatics*, p. 9. These questions are a paraphrase of what Kierkegaard wrote.

9. Søren Kierkegaard, *Philosophical Fragments*, tr. by David F. Swenson (Princeton University Press, 1936), pp. 51 ff. and 87.

10. The full German title was *Der sogenannte historische Jesus und der geschichtliche, biblische Christus.*

11. R. Bultmann, "Offenbarung und Heilsgeschehen," *Beiträge zur evangelischen Theologie*, ed. E. Wolf (Munich: Evangelischer Verlag, Albert Lampp, 1941), 7, p. 66.

12. R. Bultmann, "Preaching: Genuine and Secularized," *Religion and Culture, Essays in Honor of Paul Tillich*, ed. by Walter Leibrecht (Harper & Brothers, 1959), p. 240.

13. R. Bultmann, " A Reply to the Theses of J. Schniewind," *Kerygma and Myth*, ed. by H. W. Bartsch, tr. by Reginald H. Fuller (London: S.P.C.K., 1954), p. 112.

14. Ernst Käsemann, "The Problem of the Historical Jesus," *Essays on New Testament Themes*, tr. by W. J. Montague (London: SCM Press, Ltd., 1964), pp. 15–47.

15. *Ibid.*, p. 16.

16. *Ibid.*, p. 37.

17. Günther Bornkamm, *Jesus of Nazareth*, tr. by Irene and Fraser McLuskey (Harper & Brothers, 1960).

18. Günther Bornkamm, "Myth and Gospel," *Kerygma and History*, tr. and ed. by Carl E. Braaten and Roy A. Harrisville (Abingdon Press, 1962), p. 186.

19. Günther Bornkamm, *Jesus of Nazareth*, p. 21.

20. *Ibid.*, p. 24.

21. Cf. Ernst Fuchs, *Studies of the Historical Jesus*, tr. by Andrew Scobie (London: SCM Press, Ltd., 1964).

22. Cf. Gerhard Ebeling, *The Nature of Faith*, tr. by Ronald Gregor Smith (Muhlenberg Press, 1961); and *Word and Faith*.

23. Rudolf Bultmann, "The Primitive Christian Kerygma and the Historical Jesus," *The Historical Jesus and the Kerygmatic Christ*, p. 34.

24. Joachim Jeremias, *The Problem of the Historical Jesus*, tr. by Norman Perrin (Fortress Press, 1964), p. 18.

25. *Ibid.*, p. 20.

26. *Ibid.*, p. 23.

27. *Ibid.*, p. 24.

28. Hans Conzelmann, "Jesus Christus," *Die Religion in*

Geschichte und Gegenwart (3d edition, Tübingen: J.C.B. Mohr, 1959), 650.

29. In one of his earlier writings Karl Barth used these very words: "The resurrection of Christ, or his second coming, which is the same thing, is not a historical event." *The Word of God and the Word of Man,* tr. by Douglas Horton (Harper & Brothers, 1957), p. 90.

Chapter IV

The Historical Event of the Resurrection

1. Käsemann, "The Problem of the Historical Jesus," *Essays on New Testament Themes,* p. 25.

2. Günther Bornkamm, *Jesus of Nazareth,* p. 16.

3. Hans Conzelmann, "Jesus von Nazareth und der Glaube an den Auferstandenen," *Der historische Jesus und der kerygmatische Christus,* ed. by Helmut Ristow and Karl Matthiae (Berlin: Evangelische Verlagsanstalt, 1960), pp. 190–191.

4. Ebeling, *The Nature of Faith,* p. 60.

5. Willi Marxsen, *Anfangsprobleme der Christologie* (Kassel: Gütersloher Verlagshaus Gerd Mohn, 1960), p. 51.

6. Rudolf Bultmann, "New Testament and Mythology," *Kerygma and Myth,* p. 42.

7. *Ibid.,* p. 39.

8. *Ibid.,* p. 41.

9. Schubert Ogden, *Christ Without Myth* (Harper & Brothers, 1961), p. 136.

10. *Ibid.,* p. 136.

11. *Ibid.,* pp. 143–144.

12. *Ibid.,* p. 145.

13. *Ibid.*

14. Cf. Fritz Buri's essay "Entmythologisierung oder Entkerygmatisierung der Theologie," *Kerygma und Mythos,* Vol. II, ed. by Hans Werner Bartsch (Hamburg: Herbert Reich Evangelischer Verlag, 1952).

15. Ernst Fuchs, *Zum hermeneutischen Problem in der Theologie* (Tübingen: J.C.B. Mohr, 1959), p. 304.

16. Bultmann, "New Testament and Mythology," *loc. cit.,* p. 39. I have supplied my translation of this passage in Bultmann's essay in this sole instance. The German says, *"Wie fatal diese Argumentation ist,"* which has been translated as "But this is a dangerous procedure." I have preferred a literal translation.

17. Ebeling, *Word and Faith,* pp. 301–302. The italics in the last sentence are mine.

18. Ebeling, *The Nature of Faith,* p. 70.

19. *Ibid.,* p. 71.

20. *Ibid.*

21. Paul van Buren, *The Secular Meaning of the Gospel* (The Macmillan Company, 1963), p. 74.

22. *Ibid.,* p. 128, n. 36.

23. *Ibid.,* pp. 130–131.

24. Ludwig Wittgenstein (1889–1951) was a philosopher at the University of Cambridge. His earlier theories influenced the Vienna Circle of positivism, but his later theories began the new wave of analytic linguistic philosophy.

25. Paul van Buren, *op. cit.,* p. 132.

26. *Ibid.,* p. 133.

27. Walter Künneth, *The Theology of the Resurrection,* tr. by James W. Leitch (London: SCM Press, Ltd., 1965).

28. Wolfhart Pannenberg, *Grundzüge der Christologie* (Gütersloh: Gerd Mohn, 1964), p. 61.

29. *Ibid.,* p. 62.

30. *Ibid.,* pp. 62–69.

31. *Ibid.,* p. 70.

32. *Ibid.,* p. 71.

33. Wolfhart Pannenberg, "Did Jesus Really Rise from the Dead?" *Dialog,* Vol. 4 (1965), p. 131.

34. Pannenberg, *Grundzüge der Christologie,* pp. 79–82.

35. *Ibid.,* p. 81.

36. *Ibid.,* pp. 82–84.

37. Pannenberg, "Did Jesus Really Rise from the Dead?" *loc. cit.,* p. 131.

38. Richard R. Niebuhr, *Resurrection and Historical Reason,* p. 3.

39. Jürgen Moltmann, *Theologie der Hoffnung* (Munich: Chr. Kaiser Verlag, 1965), p. 157.

40. *Ibid.,* p. 158.

41. Hugh Anderson, *Jesus and Christian Origins* (Oxford University Press, 1964).

42. Alan Richardson, *History Sacred and Profane,* p. 212.

CHAPTER V

"HEILSGESCHICHTE" AND THE OLD TESTAMENT

1. Johann Christian Konrad von Hofmann (1810–1877) was a Lutheran theologian at Erlangen University who developed

a theology of *Heilsgeschichte*. He proposed in his two-volume work *Prophecy and Fulfillment* that we should read the Bible as an inspired history moving from the Old Testament period of prophecy to its goal of fulfillment in Christ. Bultmann dismisses Hofmann's view as theologically irrelevant. It is but an interesting "philosophy of history" quite useless for faith. Rudolf Bultmann, "Prophecy and Fulfillment," *Essays on Old Testament Hermeneutics*, ed. by Claus Westermann (John Knox Press, 1964), pp. 55–58.

2. Quoted from Hans Joachim Kraus, *Geschichte der historisch-kritischen Erforschung des Alten Testaments von der Reformation bis zur Gegenwart* (Neukirchen: Verlag der Buchhandlung des Erziehungsvereins, 1956), p. 351. Translation mine.

3. Friedrich Schleiermacher, *The Christian Faith*, paragraph 132, p. 610.

4. The exchange of views between von Rad and Conzelmann can be found in *Evangelische Theologie*, 24, 3 and 7, 1964.

5. The title of Bultmann's essay in *The Old Testament and Christian Faith*, ed. by B. W. Anderson (Harper & Row, Publishers, Inc., 1963).

6. Cf. von Rad's reference to this point in Vol. II of his *Theologie des Alten Testaments* (Munich: Chr. Kaiser Verlag) p. 403, n. 1.

7. Heinrich Bornkamm, *Luther und das Alte Testament* (Tübingen: J. C. B. Mohr, 1948).

8. James M. Robinson, "The Historicality of Biblical Language," Bernhard W. Anderson, ed., *The Old Testament and Christian Faith*, p. 150.

9. *Ibid.*, p. 151.

10. *Ibid.*, pp. 154–155.

11. Gerhard von Rad, *Old Testament Theology*, Vol. I (Edinburgh: Oliver & Boyd, Ltd., 1962), pp. 106–108.

12. Cf. Franz Hesse's article by this title, "Kerygma oder geschichtliche Wirklichkeit?" *Zeitschrift für Theologie und Kirche*, 57 (1960), 17–26. See also his "Die Erforschung der Geschichte Israels als theologische Aufgabe," *Kerygma und Dogma*, 4 (1958), 1–19.

13. Typical of this way of thinking is Baumgärtel's statement, "The Old Testament facts are not facts at all, and thus the Old Testament history of salvation is not a history of salvation at all." Quoted from Walther Eichrodt, "Is Typological Exegesis an Appropriate Method?" *Essays on Old Testament Hermeneutics*, p. 236.

14. Friedrich Baumgärtel, "The Hermeneutical Problem of the Old Testament," *Essays on Old Testament Hermeneutics,* p. 135.

15. *Ibid.,* p. 145.

16. *Ibid.,* p. 152.

17. Claus Westermann, "Remarks on the Theses of Bultmann and Baumgärtel," *Essays on Old Testament Hermeneutics,* p. 133.

18. Rolf Rendtorff, "Geschichte und Überlieferung," *Studien zur Theologie der alttestamentlichen Überlieferungen,* ed. by Rolf Rendtorff and Klaus Koch (Neukirchen: Verlag der Buchhandlung des Erziehungsvereins, 1961), p. 89.

19. *Ibid.,* p. 89.

20. *Ibid.,* p. 93.

21. Gerhard von Rad, "Typological Interpretation of the Old Testament," *Essays on Old Testament Hermeneutics,* p. 36.

22. Karl Barth, *Church Dogmatics,* Vol. I, Part 2 (Charles Scribner's Sons, 1956), p. 72.

23. *Ibid.,* p. 103.

24. In English we have only the first volume of *The Witness of the Old Testament to Christ* by Wilhelm Vischer, tr. by A. B. Crabtree (London: Lutterworth Press, 1949).

25. *Ibid.,* p. 7.

26. Karl Barth, *Church Dogmatics,* p. 80.

27. Luther laid down the rule that we should search the books of Holy Scripture *"ob sie Christum treiben oder nicht,"* that is, whether they convey Christ. Luther applied this rule with respect to each *book* of the Bible, not to each *text*.

28. Rudolf Bultmann, "Prophecy and Fulfillment," *loc. cit.,* p. 54.

29. *Ibid.,* pp. 62, 63, 67, 71.

30. Rudolf Bultmann, *History and Eschatology* (Edinburgh: The University Press, 1957), p. 36.

31. Rudolf Bultmann, "Prophecy and Fulfillment," *loc. cit.,* p. 73.

32. Rudolf Bultmann, "The Significance of the Old Testament for the Christian Faith," *loc. cit.,* p. 17.

33. *Ibid.*

34. *Ibid.,* p. 16.

35. *Ibid.,* p. 22.

36. *Ibid.,* p. 31.

37. *Ibid.,* p. 32.

38. Walther Eichrodt, "Is Typological Exegesis an Appropriate Method?" *loc. cit.,* p. 227.

39. Gerhard von Rad, "Typological Interpretation of the Old Testament," *loc. cit.,* p. 36.

40. Pannenberg, "Redemptive Event and History," *Essays on Old Testament Hermeneutics,* p. 327.

41. Gerhard von Rad, "Typological Interpretation of the Old Testament," *loc. cit.,* p. 25.

42. *Ibid.,* p. 27.

43. Walther Zimmerli, "Promise and Fulfillment," *Essays on Old Testament Hermeneutics,* p. 97.

44. *Ibid.,* pp. 111–112.

45. *Ibid.,* p. 114.

46. Gerhard von Rad, "Typological Interpretation of the Old Testament," *loc. cit.,* p. 39.

CHAPTER VI

HERMENEUTICS OF THE WORD AND CHURCH

1. Cf. *The New Hermeneutic, New Frontiers in Theology,* edited by James M. Robinson and John B. Cobb, Jr. (Harper & Row, Publishers, Inc., 1964), Vol. II. See also "How New Is the New Hermeneutic?" by Carl E. Braaten, *Theology Today,* July, 1965, 218–235. Parts of this article have been reworked in this book.

2. O. F. Bollnow, "Wilhelm Dilthey," *Die Religion in Geschichte und Gegenwart* (Tübingen: J.C.B. Mohr, 1958), 3d edition.

3. Cf. Hans Georg Gadamer, *Wahrheit und Methode* (Tübingen: J.C.B. Mohr, 1960), p. 209.

4. Cf. Rudolf Bultmann, *History and Eschatology* (Edinburgh: The University Press, 1957), pp. 111 ff.

5. Rudolf Bultmann, "The Problem of Hermeneutics," *Essays,* tr. by James C. G. Greig (London: SCM Press, Ltd., 1955), p. 238.

6. *Ibid.,* p. 256.

7. Gadamer, *op. cit.,* pp. 314–315.

8. Gerhard Ebeling, "Word of God and Hermeneutics," *Word and Faith,* p. 319.

9. James Robinson, *The New Hermeneutic,* p. 6.

10. *Ibid.,* p. 67.

11. Cf. Ebeling's essay on Bonhoeffer, "The 'Non-religious Interpretation of Biblical Concepts,' " *Word and Faith,* pp. 98–161.

12. Heinrich Ott, *Theology and Preaching,* tr. by Harold Knight (The Westminster Press, 1965).

13. *Ibid.*, p. 17.

14. *Ibid.*, p. 21.

15. Heinrich Ott, "What Is Systematic Theology?" *The Later Heidegger and Theology, New Frontiers in Theology*, edited by James M. Robinson and John B. Cobb, Jr. (Harper & Row, Publishers, Inc., 1963), Vol. I, p. 79.

16. *Ibid.*, p. 82.

17. This is especially clear in two of his essays: "The Necessity of the Doctrine of the Two Kingdoms," *Word and Faith*, pp. 386–406; and "Verantworten des Glaubens in Begegnung mit dem Denken M. Heideggers," *Zeitschrift für Theologie und Kirche*, September, 1961.

18. Ott, "What Is Systematic Theology?" *loc. cit.*, p. 199.

19. Cf. for example, the complaints against Ott by Karl Barth's old friend Eduard Thurneysen, in "Warum nicht Gollwitzer?" *Evangelische Theologie*, 22 (1962), 273–275.

20. Cf. Wolfhart Pannenberg, "Hermeneutik und Universalgeschichte," *Zeitschrift für Theologie und Kirche*, 60 (1963), 98.

21. Wolfhart Pannenberg, "The Crisis of the Scripture-Principle in Protestant Theology," *Dialog*, Vol. 2 (1963), 312.

22. *Ibid.*

23. *Ibid.*, 313.

24. Gerhard Ebeling, "The Significance of the Critical Historical Method for Church and Theology in Protestantism," *Word and Faith*, p. 34.

25. Gerhard Ebeling, *Kirchengeschichte als Geschichte der Auslegung der Heiligen Schrift* (Tübingen: J.C.B. Mohr, 1947).

26. Ebeling, "The Significance of the Critical Historical Method," *loc. cit.*, pp. 36–37. Ebeling as a church historian, of course, knows that actually the Reformers never dispensed with the Sacraments as such; they retained much that in principle is not essential to a church of the Word alone. There is much of the medieval eggshell that clung to the pure church of the Word that was in the process of being hatched. This is a familiar but specious way of interpreting the intention of the Reformers. It makes the historian as a crypto-systematician wiser than the subjects whom he interprets.

27. James M. Robinson, "Interpretation of Scripture in Biblical Studies Today," *Ecumenical Dialogue at Harvard*, edited by Samuel H. Miller and G. Ernest Wright (The Belknap Press of Harvard University Press, 1964), pp. 90–93.

28. Cf. the following essays by Käsemann: "Ministry and Community in the New Testament" and "The Canon of the

New Testament and the Unity of the Church," both in *Essays on New Testament Themes;* and "Paulus und der Frühkatholizismus," *Exegetische Versuche und Besinnungen,* Vol. II (Göttingen: Vandenhoek & Ruprecht, 1964).

29. Käsemann, "The Canon of the New Testament and the Unity of the Church," *loc. cit.,* p. 103.

30. One has only to take account of Hans Küng's discussion of Käsemann's position to realize that the Protestant in this case is caught with his ecumenical pants down. In fact, Küng labels Käsemann's selection of a part of the New Testament as "heresy." Here is Küng's conclusion: "What actually is at issue here? Nothing but the fundamental renunciation of a comprehensive understanding and a serious acceptance of the *whole* New Testament in favor of a serried *selection,* that is, the fundamental rejection of a 'Catholic' understanding of Scripture in favor of 'heresy.' " Hans Küng, *Structures of the Church,* tr. by Salvator Attanasio (Thomas Nelson & Sons, 1964), p. 161.

31. Karl Barth, *Church Dogmatics,* Vol. I, Part 1, tr. by G. T. Thomas (Charles Scribner's Sons, 1936), p. 308.

32. John A. T. Robinson, *Liturgy Coming to Life* (The Westminster Press, 1964), p. 10.

33. *Ibid.,* pp. 25–26.

CHAPTER VII
ESCHATOLOGY AND HISTORY

1. Johannes Weiss, *Die Predigt Jesu vom Reiche Gottes.* 1892.

2. See Martin Werner, *The Formation of Christian Dogma,* tr. by S. G. F. Brandon (Harper & Brothers, 1957); and Fritz Buri, *Dogmatik als Selbstverständnis des christlichen Glaubens* (Bern: P. Haupt, 1956).

3. John Wick Bowman, "From Schweitzer to Bultmann," *Theology Today,* July, 1954, 11, 165.

4. See Dodd's *The Coming of Christ* (Cambridge: The University Press, 1954).

5. The pertinent books are: Joachim Jeremias, *The Parables of Jesus,* tr. by S. H. Hooke (Charles Scribner's Sons, 1955); W. G. Kümmel, *Promise and Fulfilment,* tr. by Dorothea M. Barton (London: SCM Press, Ltd., 1957); Oscar Cullmann, *Christ and Time,* tr. by Floyd V. Filson (The Westminster Press, 1950).

6. See John Marsh's exegetically well founded criticisms of Cullmann's idea of eternity in *The Fulness of Time* (Harper & Brothers, 1952), pp. 174–181.

7. See Rudolf Bultmann's critical review of Cullmann's book, "History of Salvation and History," *Existence and Faith,* tr. by Schubert Ogden (Meridian Books, 1960), pp. 226–240; also Erich Dinkler, "Earliest Christianity," *The Idea of History in the Ancient Near East,* ed. by Robert C. Dentan (London: Oxford University Press, 1955), pp. 169–214; Karl Gerhard Steck, *Die Idee der Heilsgeschichte, Theologische Studien,* ed. by Karl Barth and Max Geiger (Zollikon: Evangelischer Verlag, 1959), No. 56.

8. Rudolf Bultmann, *History and Eschatology,* pp. 38–55.

9. See Bultmann, "Jesus and Paul," *Existence and Faith,* pp. 183–201.

10. See Jürgen Moltmann's excellent analysis and critique of the effect of Heidegger's concept of time on theology in "Exegese und Eschatologie der Geschichte," *Evangelische Theologie* (1962), 22, 48–52.

11. Ernst Käsemann, "Die Anfänge christlicher Theologie," *Exegetische Versuche und Besinnungen,* Vol. II (Göttingen: Vandenhoek und Ruprecht, 1964), p. 100.

12. *Ibid.,* p. 95. The English translation of this passage from Käsemann's essay has been made by James M. Robinson in his article "Basic Shifts in German Theology," *Interpretation,* 16 (1962), 89.

13. Gerhard Ebeling, "Der Grund christlicher Theologie," *Zeitschrift für Theologie und Kirche,* 58 (1961), 225–244; Ernst Fuchs, "Über die Aufgabe einer christlichen Theologie," *ibid.,* pp. 245–267.

14. Ernst Käsemann, "Zum Thema der urchristlichen Apokalyptik," *Zeitschrift für Theologie und Kirche,* 59 (1962), 257–284.

15. The best evidence of this can be found in his article "Eschatologie" in *Die Religion in Geschichte und Gegenwart,* 680–689.

16. Tillich, *Systematic Theology,* Vol. I, p. 271.

17. The title of Tillich's latest volume of sermons is *The Eternal Now* (Charles Scribner's Sons, 1963).

18. Both are published under the title "Christ—the Hope of the World," *The Ecumenical Review,* Vol. VII (January, 1955), 127–150.

19. For example, Emil Brunner, *The Eternal Hope,* tr. by

Harold Knight (The Westminster Press, 1954); J. E. Fison, *The Christian Hope* (London: Longmans, Green and Co., Inc., 1954); T. A. Kantonen, *The Christian Hope* (Muhlenberg Press, 1954); Paul S. Minear, *Christian Hope and the Second Coming* (The Westminster Press, 1954).

20. Rudolf Bultmann, *History and Eschatology,* pp. 154–155.

21. Helmut Gollwitzer discusses Ernst Bloch's atheistic interpretation of religion in *The Existence of God as Confessed by Faith,* tr. by James W. Leitch (The Westminster Press, 1965), pp. 97–107.

22. Heinrich Ott, *Eschatologie, Theologische Studien,* No. 53; Walter Kreck, *Die Zukunft des Gekommenen* (Munich: Chr. Kaiser Verlag, 1961).

Indexes

Indexes

NAMES

SUBJECTS